OUR LIFE IN THE CHURCH

OUR LIFE
IN THE CHURCH

Faith and Life Series

BOOK EIGHT

Ignatius Press, San Francisco
Catholics United for the Faith, New Rochelle

Nihil Obstat: Francis J. Mc Aree, S.T.D.
                Censor Librorum
Imprimatur: + Joseph T. O'Keefe, D.D.
                Vicar General, New York

Director: Rev. Msgr. Eugene Kevane, Ph.D.
Assistant Director and General Editor: Patricia I. Puccetti, M.A.
Writer: Martha Schaeffer Long

Catholics United for the Faith, Inc., and Ignatius Press gratefully acknowledge the guidance and assistance of Reverend Monsignor Eugene Kevane, former Director of the Pontifical Catechetical Institute, Diocese of Arlington, Virginia, in the production of this series. The series intends to implement the authentic approach in Catholic catechesis given to the Church in the recent documents of the Holy See and in particular the Conference of Joseph Cardinal Ratzinger on ''Sources and Transmission of Faith''.

CONTENTS

APPENDIX

PART ONE

The Church

CHAPTER 1

Christ's Abiding Presence

"I will not leave you orphans"
(Jn 14:18).

These overwhelming words of Our Lord Jesus at the Last Supper ring in our ears as they have rung through the ages. Christ suffered the agony of his Passion and the ignominious death on the Cross because of his love for us. He said, "Greater love has no man than this, that a man lay down his life for his friends" (Jn 15:13). He died to save us from sin and to show us the way to glory through taking up our daily crosses. He wanted to lift us up to himself.

But what would happen after Jesus' death, Resurrection and final Ascension into Heaven? His friends feared what would happen. Would he leave only a memory of those days when his friends and disciples so keenly felt the joy of his presence among them? Imagine what it would be like if you had been among them and known him.

The disciples on the road to Emmaus said to each other after Jesus parted from them, "Did not our hearts burn within us as he talked to us?" (Lk 24:32). That question shows something of the mysterious power his words and his presence must have had. Was this loving holy presence of Jesus to be gone for ever from the earth? There would be a terrible desolation without him. No, Jesus Christ himself said, "I will be with you always even to the end of the world" (Mt 28:20).

A good father does not forget his children when he goes away. He wants to make sure that they will be taken care of in his absence. Jesus' love for us was so great that it did not stop even with dying for each one of us personally. He wanted to continue to take care of us.

How did Jesus provide for us? How is he with us always?

The words to the apostles "I will not leave you orphans" were immediately preceded by the promise that the Holy Spirit would be sent to them. God the Father would send "the Spirit of Truth", also called the Spirit of Love, or the Fire of Love, who would be the soul of his Church. Christ has left us that Church. Christ is the eternal Shepherd and has appointed a chief shepherd and other shepherds to represent him in the care of his flock.

Christ Founded His Church

It is recorded in the Gospels that many times Christ spoke of the Church in parables or implicitly. But twice he spoke of her explicitly.

1. First Christ said to Peter in front of the other apostles, "You are Peter and upon this rock I will build my Church, and the powers of death shall not prevail against it" (Mt 16:18). What did he mean when he said he will build *his* Church? He obviously meant what he said. He said so with some emphasis and solemnity.

2. In another passage (Mt 18:17) Jesus says that, if disputes and grievances cannot be settled charitably among those involved, they should be brought to the Church and the Church will make the ultimate decision about the argument. If then the offender "refuses to listen to the Church, let him be to you as a Gentile, and a tax collector". In other words in the mind of Christ, the Church was to be the final judge and arbiter of whatever questions might arise among his followers.

In both these passages Jesus clearly speaks of his intention to begin his Church. He in fact continues immediately after both these declarations to say to his apostles, "Whatever you bind on earth shall be bound in Heaven . . ." (Mt 16:19; 18:18). This is an almost shocking statement. Christ here was actually giving power over Heaven, to a select group of twelve apostles. It was a divine authority that he gave them.

So we see that the Church was willed by Christ, founded and built by Christ. He said, "I will build my Church." The Church is therefore of divine origin. She is different from any other society or community. No other human society can claim the presence and guidance of the Holy Spirit. The Church is not man-made or merely human. This is why we call the Church a supernatural mystery.

The Church Has a Structure

Her members are human, to be sure. And God who understands and provides for our needs, made us to live together in community. "It is not good that man should be alone" (Gen 2:18). He also takes into account the universal characteristics of human societies: for instance, that a society needs leaders, a hierarchy (or assistant leaders), members, rules, and some kind of organization. Without these, societies would become chaotic. It belongs to the nature of things that societies cannot function without structure. We see this in a family or in a sports team.

Or take the example of an orchestra. There is a conductor. Then there is the first violinist, who leads the string section, while the clarinetist leads the woodwinds. It is also necessary to have all sorts of instruments, not just one or one kind. Some—for example, the cymbals—may seem to have an insignificant role. But what would it sound like at the crucial moment without them? They are truly necessary for the music to sound complete.

Using the example of an orchestra as a comparison to the Church we can say that the structure of the whole orchestra, the conductor, the various leaders, the players, and the instruments are absolutely necessary for the sake of the music. The music cannot come through harmoniously without a structure. On the other hand, they would all be mute without the music. The music is the soul of the whole thing. So it is with the Church. The Holy Spirit—the Spirit of Truth, the Spirit of Love—is, as it were, the music. He is the very soul of the Church. So Christ has promised us this heavenly music, the Holy Spirit sent by the Father, coming through the structure of the institutional Church. In the case of the Church, the fundamental structure itself is willed by Christ.

Christ's Church

Through, with, and in the Church, Christ Our Lord is present. She is *his* Church. She is not someone's idea of what is needed, or the decision of some group that it would be a sensible thing to found a community and elect leaders. She is not a mere human construction, something created by man which can be reorganized at will. It is Christ himself who has founded his Church and divinely appointed his apostles and their successors. He has called each one of us through baptism to play a vital role as a living member of the Church. It is through the Church that we receive the sacraments. It is through the Church that we receive the Holy Eucharist, which is the staggering gift of his presence among us.

In this section of the book we will study this Church of Christ in detail—what she is, what she teaches, her order, her members and what, in brief, has been her history.

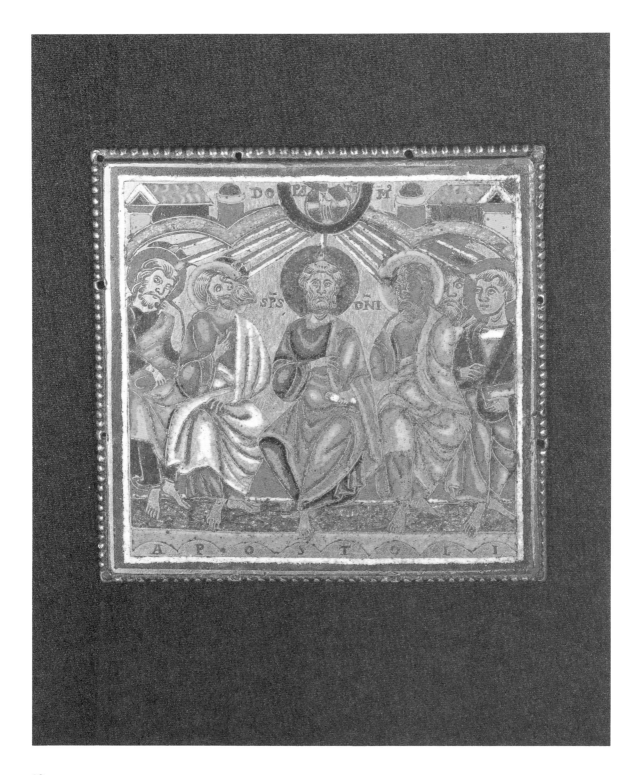

CHAPTER 2

The Birth of the Church

"But . . . the Holy Spirit, whom the Father will send in my name, he will teach you all things, and bring to your remembrance all that I have said to you" (Jn 14:26).

These words of Our Lord, taken from his last discourse on the night before he died, contain his promise to send the Holy Spirit to give life to his Church. In the second chapter of the Acts of the Apostles we find St. Luke's account of this great event.

The descent of the Holy Spirit upon the apostles is called Pentecost and is considered the "birthday" of the Church. On this day the Holy Spirit appeared—in the form of fire—to the small community of Jesus' followers who had gathered in the upper room in Jerusalem— the first members of the Catholic Church. The Holy Spirit gave them the grace to preach the Good News of Jesus Christ so that the Church might increase and spread as Our Lord had commanded.

Pentecost was, however, only the final step in God's plan to establish his Church on earth. For thousands of years God had been preparing for this moment when his Church would finally be manifested to the world. There were, in fact, three stages in the establishment of the Church. It was prefigured in the Old Testament, made present during Christ's life on earth, and made manifest to the world on Pentecost.

The beginnings of the Church can be found in the promises God made to Adam after the Fall. God made further promises to Noah after the flood. In fact, the ark, which saved Noah and his family from the waters of the flood, is a symbol of the Church.

With Abraham and the formation of the chosen people, the origins of the Church become more clear. At this stage, God made a covenant with Abraham and his descendants to be their protector. This was the beginning of the "*ekklesia*"—the people set apart—that they might become holy.

As we follow the history of the chosen people—the Jews—we see even more clearly the early stages of the Church. When Moses led his people out of Egypt God renewed his covenant (now with the whole people), making them into a true nation. Now they began to worship God through a formal religion, with special ceremonies and a certain code of moral behavior, namely, the Ten Commandments. They now prefigured what Peter said of the Christian Church. They were a "chosen race, a royal priesthood, a holy nation, God's own people. . ." (1 Pet 2:9).

In the laws of the Old Covenant we can see the Church prefigured. This chosen race, a people set apart, was established with a sacred priesthood to celebrate their Liturgy. This worship of God was a corporate act, that is, the action of the whole people. At the head of the chosen race was God himself, but on earth Moses was his representative. Under Moses there was a hierarchical structure. Aaron and his sons were priests and all other priests would come from their descendants, members of the tribe of Levi. All of this was so that this ''church'' could fulfill its purpose—to make the people holy.

Later in their history God formed his people into a kingdom, renewing his covenant with David, who foreshadowed the eternal King— Christ. This chosen people was now firmly established, with God as King and David as his earthly vicar, a foreshadowing of the relationship of Christ and the head of his Church.

God continued to reveal himself and his will to the people through the prophets. Through these prophets God prepared this chosen race for the coming of the Savior, through whom the Church would be firmly established.

''In many and various ways God spoke of old to our fathers by the prophets, but in these last days he has spoken to us by a Son, whom he appointed the heir of all things; through whom he also created the world'' (Heb 1:1−2).

When the Son of God became a man and made his dwelling among us, the Church was actually established on earth. Christ laid the foundations as he preached during his public life. First he chose twelve disciples, called apostles, who were to be the leaders of the Church. They were from different backgrounds: some were uneducated—simple fishermen; another was educated and held a position in the government—a tax collector. Jesus spent a great part of his time teaching and forming this group of specially chosen men, the Twelve Apostles. To the multitude he taught in parables, but to the Twelve he spoke directly, ''The secret of the Kingdom of God is given to you, but to those outside everything is in parables'' (Mk 4:12). His intention clearly was that they would be carriers of his message: ''Follow me and I will make you fishers of men'' (Mk 1:17).

One of the apostles, Peter, was chosen by Our Lord to be the leader of all and to be Jesus' representative on earth. After Peter demonstrated great faith, Our Lord said to him, ''. . . you are Peter, and on this rock I will build my Church and the powers of death shall not prevail against it. I will give you the keys of the kingdom . . . '' (Mt 16:18−19). By giving Peter the ''keys'' Our Lord signified the authority that was given to Peter.

At the Last Supper, the night before he died, Our Lord prayed for unity in his Church. He prayed ''not . . . for these only, but also for those who believe in me through their word, that they may all be one . . .'' (Jn 17:20−21). He also promised to send them the Holy Spirit so that they might recall all that Jesus had taught them and be able to teach his message.

Church Teaching

''The origin and growth of the Church are symbolized by the blood and water which flowed from the open side of the crucified Jesus'' (LG, 3).

Through these words Jesus made it clear that his Church was to continue after his death.

When Our Lord ascended into Heaven, the basic structure of the Church was complete. By his death he merited for us the graces of salvation. We call this the *deposit of grace*, which is dispensed to us through the sacraments of the Church. The truths that Our Lord revealed during his three years of public life and during the forty days after the Resurrection were given in a special way to the apostles so that they might teach others. This we call the *deposit of faith*.

The last instruction of Our Lord to the apostles, according to St. Matthew's Gospel, mandated the mission of his Church. On the day of the Ascension Our Lord told his followers, led by St. Peter and the apostles, "Go therefore and make disciples of all nations, baptizing them in the name of the Father and of the Son and of the Holy Spirit, teaching them to observe all that I have commanded you; and lo, I am with you always, to the close of the age" (Mt 28:19−20). The Church, in other words, must manifest herself to the world.

Ten days later, while the leaders of the Church were gathered in prayer, this manifestation began. The Holy Spirit, promised by Our Lord, descended upon them, and they were filled with the Spirit of Love and Truth, who gave them the grace to go forth and preach. On this day Peter, as the leader of the Church, preached his first sermon to the Jewish pilgrims gathered in Jerusalem, urging them to be baptized. "Those who received his word were baptized and there were added that day about three thousand souls" (Acts 2:41). At this point the Church began her mission to the world.

Since that first Pentecost, the Church has grown and spread into every part of the world. The same Church that was prefigured in the Old Testament, formed by Christ, and manifested to the world on Pentecost still exists today, leading men to God. The Church was finally established as "a chosen race, a royal priesthood, a holy nation . . . who in times past were not a people, but now are the People of God" (1 Pet 2:9−10).

Words to Know:

> Pentecost   vicar   ekklesia
> deposit of grace   deposit of faith

Q. 1   *What is the Church?*
The Church is the community of true Christians, that is, baptized persons who profess the faith and teaching of Jesus Christ, who participate in his sacraments, and who obey the pastors whom he has appointed.

Q. 2   *By whom was the Church founded?*
The Church was founded by Jesus Christ, who gathered his faithful followers into one community, placed it under the direction of the apostles with St. Peter as its head, and gave it its sacrifice, its sacraments, and the Holy Spirit, who gives it life.

CHAPTER 3

The Nature of the Church

"By her relationship with Christ, the Church is a kind of sacrament or sign of intimate union with God, and of the unity of all mankind" *(LG, 1).*

We have seen that the Church is a society that was carefully formed by God and began its mission at Pentecost. This society is composed of those baptized persons who profess the faith taught by Jesus Christ and handed down by his apostles and their successors. The members participate in the sacraments given to us by Our Lord, and are united with their bishops under the leadership of the Pope.

In order to understand the nature of the Church more fully, we need to examine three significant points: (1) the Church as the Mystical Body of Christ, (2) the marks of the Church, and (3) the reasons Christ established his Church.

Images in the New Testament

Many images used in the New Testament help us to understand the Church. A number of these arise from Our Lord's own words. Christ frequently spoke of the Kingdom that will be established on earth and finally completed in Heaven. Several parables, like that of the mustard seed, use this image, showing us how the Kingdom will grow and flourish on earth, or how the wicked and the just will live together in the world but will finally be separated at the end of time. If we reflect on this image, we can see how it pertains to the Church.

In other places Christ uses the image of the sheepfold. We, the faithful, are the sheep, led by human shepherds on earth but most perfectly by the Good Shepherd, Christ himself. In still other places Our Lord uses the images of the vineyard, a building, and his bride to represent the Church. How would these be images of the Church? You may need to use your New Testament to help you.

The Mystical Body of Christ

One of the most beautiful images is that of the Church as the Body of Christ. The roots of this image can also be found in the words of Christ. When Our Lord was speaking of the Last Judgment, he told us that we would be judged in part on the basis of our charity toward others—feeding the hungry, clothing the naked, giving drink to the thirsty, and so on. He concludes by saying, "Truly I say to you, as you did it to one of the least of these my brethren, you did it to me" (Mt 25:40). In other words, we serve Christ by serving others.

In another place, when Jesus sent the disciples out to preach in his name, he said, "He who hears you hears me, and he who rejects you, rejects me . . ." (Lk 10:16). From both of these passages, we see that Christ in some way identifies his followers—the Church—with himself.

There is another passage (Acts 9:1–5) in which the words of Christ are recorded. Not long after Pentecost a man named Saul of Tarsus was fanatically hounding and pursuing the early Church. "I was persecuting the Church of God", he later admitted (1 Cor 15:9). One day on the road to Damascus he was knocked off his horse by a light from Heaven and heard mysterious words. A voice said, "Saul, Saul, why do you persecute me? . . . I am Jesus of Nazareth, whom you are persecuting." How was it that Saul (later St. Paul) was persecuting Christ by persecuting his Church? Did it amount to the same thing? What was meant by these words?

For the rest of his life St. Paul would think about these words telling him that Christ and his Church are one. This was such a great mystery that its meaning seemed inexhaustible. He later developed this image of the Church as the Body of Christ in his first letter to the Corinthians, his letter to the Ephesians, and in many other letters.

Our physical bodies have many different parts, which are arranged so that they can work together. All of these parts—eyes, ears, hands, feet, heart, lungs, and so on—form *one* body, and each part must work for the good of the whole. If one part of the body suffers, the other parts share in this pain, while the healthy parts must come to the assistance of the sick parts. If one part—such as an infected limb—threatens the health of the whole body, it may need to be removed.

As St. Paul tells us, the same is true of the Church. The individual members of the Church must help their fellow members. A sin committed by one member hurts the whole. One saint lifts up the whole. "If one member suffers, all suffer together; if one member is honored, all rejoice together" (1 Cor 12:26). Sometimes it is even necessary to remove one member from the Church in order that the whole may remain healthy.

Furthermore, each of the many organs of the body has its own specific function and is arranged in some kind of order. Each has its own task. The eye cannot and should not want to do what the ear does. The hand cannot and should not want to do what the feet do. The same is true of the Church. There are many individuals in the Church occupying special positions and exercising special functions, but all are united in one whole under Christ. The head of this Body is Christ. St. Paul reminds us, "He is the head of the body, the Church . . ." (Col 1:18). It is Christ who unites this Body and whose life we share. We are joined together by the Holy Spirit who is personally present throughout the Church.

The Pope is the *visible* head of the Church, representing Christ. The bishops with the Pope teach, sanctify, and rule in the name of Christ. The priests and deacons assist in this work. Lay people, who make up the bulk of the Church, have their special tasks within the Body of Christ. They may, for instance, be the hands that take care of children in their families or help the poor. They may be the feet that go to visit the sick. They may be the tongues that teach their children the ways of God or spread the Word of God to others in the world. They may be defenders of the faith, like St. Thomas More. Each one has his special vocation, and all work for the one Body of Christ. All are called to holiness.

Again, the individual parts of the body form one living organism, which requires nourishment to grow and mature. The Body of Christ, like the human body, must be nurtured constantly by the graces that are received through the sacraments.

Calling the church a "body", however, is not just a figure of speech. The Church is truly the Mystical Body of Christ. *Mystical* here means spiritual. It is also called mystical to remind us of the supernatural character of this society, which is both human and divine. Unlike purely human organizations, the ultimate purpose of the Church is salvation. The goal is Heaven. The Church helps us to know, love, and serve God in this life so that we can be united with him for ever in the next.

Marks of the Church

The Church, as we have seen, is a visible institution made up of human beings united with Christ as the invisible head. Since the earliest centuries, Christians have believed that there are four signs, or *marks*, by which the true Church can be recognized. These marks are included in the Nicene Creed: "We believe in one, holy, catholic, and apostolic Church."

Let us now examine what each of these four marks means.

One

The *unity* in the Church is striking and is probably the clearest of the marks. This unity is found in three areas.

First, there is the unity of belief. The Church teaches the same doctrines everywhere and always. Throughout the world the members of the Church profess this one faith. The clearest statements of this faith are in the creeds, particularly the Apostles' Creed and the Nicene Creed. There is also unity of moral teaching, based on the Ten Commandments and the teachings of Jesus Christ. These doctrinal and moral beliefs have through the ages always been and will always remain the same.

Second, the Church is one through her unity of worship and Liturgy. There is one sacrifice, the Mass, by which all members are united in worshipping God. The Church is united also in receiving the Eucharist and other sacraments, by which all share in the life of Christ. While there is absolute unity in the *essentials* of worship, there is rich variety in the rituals and ceremonies that surround them, as we shall see later in our studies.

Third, there is unity of government in the Church. All members submit themselves to one divine authority, Christ. Christ promised us that there would be ". . . one flock, [and] one shepherd" (Jn 10:16). The shepherd is Christ, and he is represented by his Vicar on earth, the Pope. The bishops, successors of the apostles, are shepherds. The Pope is the supreme shepherd, and he, together with them, rules the Body of Christ. Christ knew that any community needed a leader to survive, so he appointed Peter to be his visible representative. It is Peter's successor and those bishops in union with him who now govern the Church. We are united to our bishop, and he in turn is united to the Pope.

Holy

The second mark of the Church is *holiness*. The Church is holy in her origin, first of all, because her Founder, Jesus Christ, is holy and is the source of all holiness. The Church is holy also in her purpose, which is the sanctification and salvation of all her members. She has all the means at her disposal to make her members holy. Her sacraments are also holy because they lead to holiness.

Finally, the Church is holy in those of her members who open themselves to grace. Throughout history, the Church has been manifested in the holiness of many men and women who have wholeheartedly accepted Christ and his Church. These *saints*, both canonized and uncanonized, are living proofs that the Church is holy. Christ said, ''By their fruits you shall know them.'' We can see the fruits of the Church in her saints.

It is important to remember that the holiness of the Church does not mean that all members of the Church are holy. Far from it, unfortunately. Most of us fall far short of holiness and many times even fall into sin. In fact, our Church history reveals that there have been many who have led ''unholy'' lives. But sin is the result of imperfections in our human nature, not in the nature of the Church herself. Despite our failures we must always strive to imitate the holiness of our Founder.

Catholic

The third mark of the Church is her *catholicity*, or universality. The Church is called catholic because she possesses the fullness of Christ's truth and revelation, and also because she is for all men and women at all times and in all places. She is not limited to one race or nation. Her members include both the rich and the poor, the educated and the uneducated, the young and the old. The Church founded by Jesus Christ, unlike the pagan religions at the time, was meant to include every human being.

This mark has become more evident as the Church has grown over the centuries. The Church has spread throughout many nations according to the command of Christ. And through her missionary work, the Church continues to manifest this mark of universality.

Apostolic

The final mark of the Church is *apostolicity*. This means that the Church originated with the apostles, upon whom Christ built his Church. We have already seen how Christ chose ''the Twelve'' to be the foundation of his Church. Apostolicity also refers to the fact that the Church is still ruled by the legitimate successors to Peter and the apostles, namely, the Pope and the bishops. In other words, the mark of apostolicity is made clear by the fact that authority in the Church can be traced in an unbroken line back to the apostles.

The Church is also apostolic in the sense that

she professes the same doctrine taught by the apostles, the deposit of faith given to the Church by Christ. This deposit of faith remains the same in all essentials. Thus the Church is founded on the apostles and the teaching given to them by Our Lord.

Why the Church?

We have seen that Christ founded the Church, his Mystical Body, and identified her by four unique and visible signs. But why did he establish this Church? Understanding this will give us a more complete grasp of the nature of the Church.

To begin with, Our Lord was on earth for only a short time. In order to offer salvation to all men, not just those living in Palestine two thousand years ago, he established his Church to continue his work. By his death Our Lord merited sufficient graces to save all men. He then entrusted to Peter and the apostles the power and the means necessary to carry out the work of salvation. Our Lord himself gave the apostles the task of administering the sacraments.

At the Last Supper, for example, they were given the power to celebrate the Holy Eucharist. After the Resurrection, they received the power to forgive sins. And on the day of the Ascension, they were directed to baptize in the name of the Trinity.

So that the Church could carry out this mission of sanctification, Christ also gave the Church the powers to govern and to teach. The power to govern is necessary so that our weakened wills will have the guidance and support needed to follow Christ and his commands. This power was indicated when Christ told first Peter, and later all of the apostles, ". . . whatever you bind on earth shall be bound in Heaven and whatever you loose on earth shall be loosed in Heaven'' (Mt 16:19). The Church, then, has the power from Christ to be the final judge determining what is necessary for salvation and sanctification.

Finally, the Church has the power from Christ to teach, so that we may know the truths that Christ has revealed to us. We have already seen that Christ instructed his apostles to go forth and teach what he had taught them. This work is carried on primarily by the successors of the apostles, the Pope and the bishops, and those who share in their authority.

In the next chapter we will consider in more detail the teaching mission of the Church and especially the sources of her teaching. In later chapters we will consider the governing and sanctifying missions of the Church.

Words to Know:

Mystical Body   apostolic   catholic

Q. 3   *Which is the Church of Jesus Christ?*
The Church of Jesus Christ subsists in the Roman Catholic Church, because she alone is one, holy, catholic, and apostolic, as he himself willed her to be.

Q. 4   Why is the Church one?

The Church is one because all of her members always have had, now have, and always will have the same faith, the same sacrifice, the same sacraments, and the same visible head, the Roman Pontiff, who is the successor of St. Peter. Thus they all together form one single body, the Mystical Body of Jesus Christ.

Q. 5   Why is the Church holy?

The Church is holy because Jesus Christ, her invisible head, and the Spirit who gives her life, are holy; because her doctrine, her sacrifice, and her sacraments are holy; because all of her members are called to make themselves holy; and because many members actually were holy, are holy now, and will be holy in the future.

Q. 6   Why is the Church catholic?

The Church is catholic, that is, universal, because she was instituted for all men, is suitable for all men, and has been extended over the whole world.

Q. 7   Why is the Church apostolic?

The Church is apostolic because she has been founded upon the apostles and on their preaching, and because she is governed by their successors, the legitimate pastors, who continue to transmit both doctrine and power without interruption or change.

Q. 8   Why did Jesus Christ institute the Church?

Jesus Christ instituted the Church so that men might have in her a secure guide and the means of holiness and eternal salvation.

Q. 9   What are the means of holiness and of eternal salvation that are found in the Church?

The means of holiness and of eternal salvation that are found in the Church are the true faith, the sacrifice, and the sacraments, together with mutual aids, such as prayer, spiritual counsel, and good example.

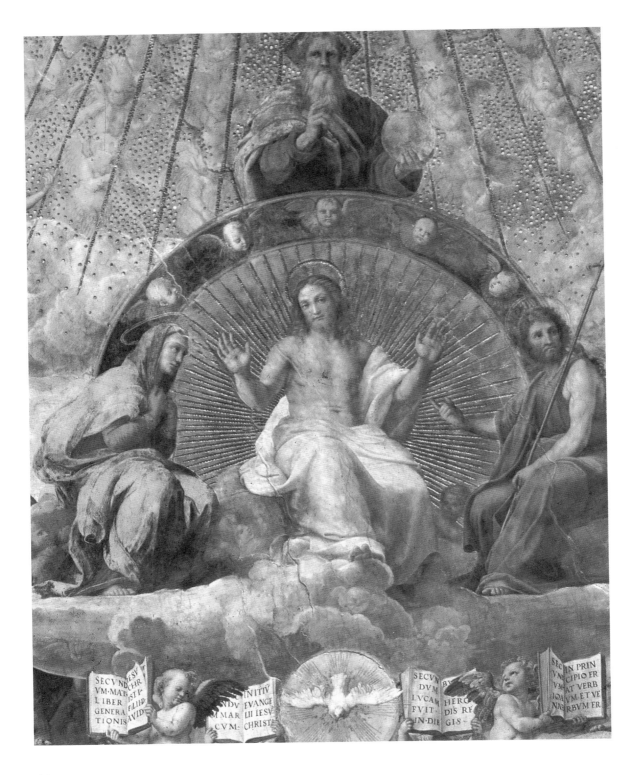

CHAPTER 4

The Teaching Church

"This gospel was to be the source of all saving truths and moral discipline. This was faithfully done: it was done by the apostles who handed on, by the spoken word of their preaching, by the example they gave, by the institutions they established, what they themselves had received" (DV, 7).

As we have already seen, Our Lord left to the Church the *deposit of faith*. His final command to the apostles was to teach all that he had instructed them. He relied on his apostles and their successors to carry his message to the world. This is made known to us today through the living voice of the Church—the Pope, the bishops, the priests—even the laity. Each of these conveys to us the message of Christ, especially the clergy, who are, by their office, the representatives of Christ. The Church bases her teaching on the deposit of faith revealed to us by God. Before we look at the source of this teaching we should first consider what is meant by *revelation*.

What Is Revelation?

Revelation literally means to "draw back the veil" or to uncover. God is primarily a mystery to us. On our own we can have only a limited knowledge of him. However, God has unveiled some of the mysteries about himself so that we might come to know and love him. He has helped us to know who he is and what he expects of us.

In other words, revelation is the communication by God to man of the truths about himself that he wants man to know but that man could never uncover alone. These truths are known as doctrines or teachings of our faith.

God did not reveal these truths about himself all at once but only gradually with the passing of time. The process of public revelation began with Abraham and ended with the death of the last apostle, St. John.

The first phase of God's revelation can be found in the Old Testament. Because this revelation took place long before the birth of Christ, we call it "pre-Christian" revelation. If we look at the Old Testament, we can see that God gradually revealed more about himself as the centuries passed.

This revelation was completed when God fully showed himself to us by becoming man and living among us. This phase is known as "Christian" revelation. It contains the truths revealed by Jesus Christ to his apostles. These revelations include the most important mysteries of our faith. Among them are the Trinity, the Incarnation, and the Eucharist.

Source of Revelation

"God graciously arranged that the things he had once revealed for the salvation of all peoples should remain in their entirety, throughout the ages, and be transmitted to all generations" (DV, 7). This sacred deposit of the Word of God has been entrusted to the Church.

There is only one single sacred deposit of the Word of God, but from it flow both Sacred Tradition and Sacred Scripture, the Bible. It is important to recognize that Tradition and Scripture are bound closely together and communicate one with the other. "Sacred Scripture is the speech of God as it is put down in writing under the breath of the Holy Spirit. And Tradition transmits in its entirety the Word of God which has been entrusted to the apostles by Christ the Lord and the Holy Spirit" (DV, 9). By means of Tradition, the books of the Bible are known to the Church, and the Scriptures are more thoroughly understood and interpreted.

Sacred Scripture, the Bible, is the written Word of God. It is made up of a collection of books written at various times by different men who wrote under God's inspiration. As we know, the Bible is made up of the Old Testament, which contains pre-Christian revelation, and the New Testament, which contains Christian revelation.

The New Testament, however, does not contain all that Jesus did and said. In fact, the various books of the New Testament were not even begun until some twenty or thirty years after the death of Christ. The apostles began to preach the message of Christ first, and only later were some of these teachings committed to writing. Scripture itself testifies to the fact that the Gospels do not include all of Jesus' words. At the end of his Gospel, St. John says, ". . . there are also many other things which Jesus did; were every one of them to be written, I suppose that the world itself could not contain the books that would be written" (Jn 21:25).

What Jesus taught his apostles was passed on to their disciples. For example, St. Polycarp of Smyrna, St. Ignatius of Antioch, and St. Clement of Rome all lived during the last part of the first century and the beginning of the second century. Because they were personally taught by the apostles, they are known as *Apostolic Fathers*. Their writings contain some of Jesus' teachings that are not explicitly found in the New Testament.

Over the centuries many varied and contradictory interpretations of the Bible have arisen. Who had the authority to decide which was the right one? It is important to note that the Church—which, as we have seen was given authority by Christ (Mt 16:19) to settle all disputes on earth—is the interpreter of Sacred Scripture. She is the custodian (or guardian) of Scripture and Tradition because she was promised the guidance of the Spirit of Truth.

The Second Vatican Council says, "Sacred Tradition and Sacred Scripture make up a single deposit of the Word of God, which is entrusted to the Church" (DV, 10).

Creeds

An important written expression of Tradition is found in the *creeds*, or statements of belief, of the Church. These creeds are summary statements of the main doctrines proposed for belief by the Church. The earliest of these dates back to very early times and is called the *Apostles' Creed*.

The *Nicene Creed*, formulated at the council of Nicaea in the fourth century, is an expansion and explanation of the Apostles' Creed. In the first creed, and in fact in the early days of the Church, most doctrines were stated in plain and simple language. Over the years questions and difficulties arose concerning many of these doctrines. The later creeds, particularly the Nicene, were written to explain more fully some of these doctrines.

Councils

A second written expression of Tradition is found in the statements of the twenty-one Ecumenical Councils of the Church. A Church council is a gathering of all the bishops—under the authority of the Pope—to discuss matters of concern to the Church. We call them *ecumenical*, meaning whole or worldwide, because they involve all the bishops. Over the centuries councils have frequently been called in response to controversies over basic doctrines of the faith. The councils have given the Church the occasion to explain more completely and accurately certain beliefs.

The earliest controversies were over the Trinity and the human and divine natures of Christ. The Council of Nicaea addressed these questions. It is evident that when there was a controversy there had to be an arbiter (or umpire) to decide what the true teaching was. Later councils addressed questions about which books were in fact inspired and thus to be included in the Bible, the nature and number of the sacraments, and the nature of the Church. The decisions of these councils clarify or define the teaching of the Church.

Fathers and Doctors Of the Church

The writings of the *Fathers* and *Doctors* of the Church are also written records of witnesses. The *Fathers of the Church* are saintly Christian writers of the early centuries of the Church who are recognized as special witnesses of the faith. Among the more well-known are the following: St. Athanasius, a bishop during the

---

The lists that follow contain some of the most important of the Fathers and Doctors of the Church.

FATHERS OF THE CHURCH

St. Ambrose

St. Augustine

St. Basil the Great

St. Benedict

St. Cyprian

St. Gregory the Great

St. Ignatius of Antioch

St. Jerome

St. John Chrysostom

St. John Damascene

St. Leo the Great

St. Paulinus of Nola

St. Polycarp

DOCTORS OF THE CHURCH

St. Albert the Great

St. Alphonsus Liguori

St. Anselm

St. Bernard of Clairvaux

St. Bonaventure

St. Catherine of Siena

St. Francis de Sales

St. John of the Cross

St. Peter Canisius

St. Robert Bellarmine

St. Teresa of Avila

St. Thomas Aquinas

late third century who defended the doctrine that Christ was both God and man against the Arian heresy; St. Augustine, a bishop of the fourth century who converted after leading a life of great sin and became one of the greatest theologians in the Church; and St. Jerome, a monk and a scholar during the fourth century who translated the Bible into Latin, the common language of the people at that time.

The *Doctors of the Church* are the saintly theologians and teachers of the later centuries whose writings are outstanding in guiding the faithful at all times. One of the foremost among these is the great Dominican St. Thomas Aquinas, who lived in Italy during the thirteenth century. Two women are included among the Doctors: St. Teresa of Avila and St. Catherine of Siena. To help you understand more about the Fathers and Doctors, you might want to choose one from the list at the end of the chapter and read about his or her life.

The writings and decrees of individual Popes are another expression of the teachings of Christ. Some of these are known as *encyclicals*, letters sent by the Pope to the bishops and the faithful, expressing the teaching of the Church on matters of faith, morals, social responsibility, and other important topics.

There is also the *"sensus fidelium"*. Literally, this phrase means "the sense of the faithful". This testimony is from what the faithful have believed over the centuries and what the saints have thought, meditated, and believed, and from the actions, prayers, etc. of the faithful.

The Church teaches us that the "whole body of the faithful who have an anointing that comes from the Holy One cannot err in matters of belief. This characteristic is shown in the supernatural appreciation of the faith (*sensus fidei*) of the whole people, when, 'from the bishops to the last of the faithful' they manifest a universal consent in matters of faith and morals" (LG, 12).

Development of Doctrine

One last point remains to be made here about the teaching of the Church. Although the deposit of faith was completed with the death of the last apostle, St. John, our understanding of it has developed over the last twenty centuries. We call this the *development of doctrine*. This is the gradual unfolding of the meaning of many things that Christ revealed to us. It is

CARDINAL NEWMAN

John Henry Cardinal Newman was born in England in 1801. He was an Anglican scholar who founded the Oxford Movement in England in order to reform the Anglican Church. In many sermons, lectures, and books, Newman expounded the "Anglo-Catholic" position. One of his most important works was a lengthy essay entitled "On the Development of Christian Doctrine", in which he discussed that part of the Church's belief that we mentioned in this chapter. His discussion of this question was the most complete treatment of it up until that time.

Eventually John Henry Newman was led to the true Church of Christ through his studies and his writings. Toward the end of his life he was made a cardinal of the Church by Pope Leo XIII.

this development of doctrine that we find in the councils of the Church, the writings of the Fathers and Doctors, and the practical experience of the faith among the faithful of the Church. Since the Holy Spirit, who continues to guide the Church, is the Spirit of Truth, any further development can never be—and never has been—in contradiction to any previous doctrine. One example to illustrate this is the definition of the doctrine of the Immaculate Conception of Our Lady. This doctrine is hinted at in Scripture (''Hail, full of grace'', Lk 1:28), was defended by St. Augustine and the later Doctors, and was part of the *sensus fidelium* for centuries. Yet it was not officially declared until 1854, by Pope Pius IX. It was not a new revelation, but rather an unfolding of one doc-trine over time. Something that is implicit in a doctrine becomes explicit, or it can be the logical consequence of a doctrine.

In this chapter we have discussed the sources of the Church's teaching. In the next chapter we will consider the authority of the Church, first, as it pertains to matters of doctrine and the teaching of the Church and, second, as it pertains to matters of discipline, the governing of the Church.

Words to Know:

revelation   Scripture   Tradition
Apostolic Fathers   Doctors of the Church
Fathers of the Church   encyclical
sensus fidelium   development of doctrine

Q. 10   *What are the truths revealed by God?*
The truths revealed by God are chiefly those summarized in the Apostles' Creed. They are called the truths of faith because we must believe them, with full faith, as taught by God, who can neither deceive nor be deceived.

Q. 11   *What is the Apostles' Creed?*
The Apostles' Creed is a profession of faith in the chief mysteries and the other truths revealed by God through Jesus Christ and his apostles and taught by the Church.

Q. 12   *What is Sacred Scripture?*
Sacred Scripture is the collection of the books written under the inspiration of God, in the Old and New Testaments, and received by the Church as the work of God himself.

Q. 13   *What is Tradition?*
Tradition is the teaching of Jesus Christ and of the apostles, done by their living voices, and transmitted from them to us by the Church without alteration.

CHAPTER 5

Authority in the Church: Teaching and Governing

". . . the Church of the living God, the pillar and bulwark of the truth" (1 Tim 3:15).

We have already seen that Christ gave his apostles a supernatural authority. He also said very solemnly: "All authority in Heaven and earth has been given to me. Go, therefore, and make disciples of all nations. . ." (Mt 28:18 − 19). He thus commissioned the apostles to teach and govern his Church, with Peter at their head.

The Pope and the bishops as their successors form the Church's *hierarchy*. A hierarchy is a ranking of those in authority. This ranking in the Church comes to us from Christ. The basic structure was laid down by him and, as the Church grew, the structure was expanded and developed.

At the head of this hierarchy is the *Pope*, the successor of St. Peter, the bishop of Rome and the head of the universal Church. The Pope has *primacy*, or the "first place", in the Church. He holds the primary authority to teach, govern, and sanctify all members of the Church. The Pope is the visible head of the Church. He represents Christ, the invisible head.

United with the Pope in governing the Church are the successors of the apostles, the bishops.

With the Pope the bishops are the most important authorities and teachers in the Church. Each bishop is a shepherd, deriving his authority from Christ, and he is responsible for governing the local church, one portion of the whole flock.

This is a pastoral work to which they dedicate themselves. It is important for us to understand that in governing they are performing a great service for our salvation. The shepherds are serving their flock, following the example of humble service which was given when Jesus washed the feet of his disciples. In fact, one of the Pope's titles is *Servus Servorum Dei*, which means "servant of the servants of God".

The Pope and the bishops exercise their authority whenever they teach the faithful in their care. Our Lord commanded his apostles to teach all that he had taught. Consequently, the bishops as their successors are fulfilling Our Lord's command when they exercise their teaching office.

Freedom, Authority, and Truth

Freedom is one of the values we most cherish. It is given to us by God and belongs to human dignity. The Church is the great defender of human freedom. You might think that because there is a teaching authority in the Church, you have less freedom. We have to think whether we mean freedom *from* reality or freedom *within* reality. Many people confuse the two. It would, for instance, be foolish to ignore the reality of the law of gravity and in the name of freedom walk off the roof of a skyscraper. You want to live in reality and not in a fantasy world, which means you want to know the truth.

So it is a gift of God's mercy to have an authority whose teaching, inspired by the Holy Spirit, is truth. Christ said: "The truth shall make you free" (Jn 8:32).

Free from Error

Because the teachings of Jesus Christ showed the way to eternal salvaton, it was extremely important that they remain in their essentials free from error. And so, Our Lord promised the Church, ". . . I am with you always, to the close of the age" (Mt 28:20). He also promised to send the Holy Spirit, who ". . . will teach you all things and bring to your remembrance all that I have said to you" (Jn 14:26).

With these and other words Our Lord left his Church with the great gift of *infallibility*. Infallibility means that the constant teaching of the Church about matters of faith or morals, as contained in the deposit of divine revelation, will be free from error. This infallibility was given to the whole Church for our benefit so that we could have certainty of truth. If we reflect briefly on the history of the Church, we will see that, even in times of great confusion, the Church's teaching remained essentially unchanged. Why? There is only one explanation —the Holy Spirit given to the Church by Christ has protected and guided the teaching authority of the Church.

Infallibility belongs to the whole Church, which means that the true Church of Christ can never teach a doctrine that is contrary to what Christ taught. But infallibility also belongs in a special way to the legitimate authorities of the Church—the Pope and the bishops. Whenever the bishops in union with the Pope teach or proclaim a matter of faith or morals as something which must be definitively held, these teachings are infallible. The bishops with the Pope reaffirm in their own dioceses the constant and certain teachings of the Church on matters of faith and morals.

Infallibility of the Pope

Infallibility also belongs in an even more special way to the successor of St. Peter, the Pope. When the Pope speaks alone is he always infallible? Obviously not. He is infallible in very definite circumstances. For instance, he is infallible when the following conditions—which are called extraordinary—are met: (1) The Pope must be speaking on matters of faith or morals; (2) he must be speaking to the *whole* Church, not a particular group or segment of the Church; (3) he must be speaking *ex cathedra* (literally, from the chair of authority), which means he is speaking as Pope, not merely as a bishop or member of the Church; and (4) he must be intending to use his authority to pronounce an unchangeable decision.

The doctrine of papal infallibility has been accepted, at least implicitly, by the Church from the beginning. It follows from Christ's promise to St. Peter making him the head of the Church. To preserve effectively the teachings of Christ, St. Peter and his successors would need this guarantee from Christ. It was not, however, *defined*, or officially declared a dogma of the Church, until 1870 at the First Vatican Council. (This represents an example of the *development of doctrine*, which we discussed in the last chapter.) Pius XII used this gift when the doctrine of Our Lady's Assumption was declared in this manner in 1950. Pius IX exercised this same authority when he defined the doctrine of the Immaculate Conception in 1854, *before* Vatican I.

Thus two Popes, almost a century apart, defined on their own authority a dogma of faith, one definition coming before and one after the dogma of papal infallibility itself was defined. This illustrates an important point. A formal, infallible definition, either by the Pope himself or by a general council of the Church, introduces no new teaching, no new doctrine. The Pope is not infallible because a general council said so; on the contrary, a general council could say so only because the Pope *is* infallible and the Church has always believed it. Our Lady's Immaculate Conception and Assumption are not true because a Pope declared them so; a Pope could declare them so because they *are* true and the Church has always believed them. Such pronouncements are simply formal and final definitions of doctrines always held by the Church.

It is important to note two things about papal infallibility. First, not everything the Pope says is infallible. He must be speaking according to the conditions laid down. It follows that his private opinions or statements, even those on faith or morals, are not infallible. It is only when he speaks as the Vicar of Christ that he can speak infallibly. Second, infallibility should not be confused with sinlessness, or *impeccability*, on the part of the Pope. The Pope is a human being and, like all of us, he can sin. There have, in fact, been times in the past when we had sinful Popes. We have been blessed in the present century with Popes whose personal holiness is great; in fact, one of them, Pius X, is a canonized saint. Thus, we sometimes expect sinlessness in the Pope and confuse this notion with infallibility.

Magisterium

The teaching office of the Church, known as the *magisterium*, is exercised in two ways: extraordinary and ordinary. The *extraordinary magisterium* refers to the solemn and formal exercise of the teaching office of the Pope and the bishops and it is always authoritative. It is infallible when the Pope alone *ex cathedra*, or a general council of the bishops of the world with the Pope, defines or proclaims a doctrine of faith or morals. We have already seen that both of these are rare; there have been twenty-one general councils in approximately two thousand years, and not every one of these councils has proclaimed infallible doctrine.

The *ordinary magisterium* refers to the normal, regular exercise of the Church's teaching office, and it, too, is always authoritative. For this, various forms of communication have been used throughout history. In our times we see the

ordinary magisterium used in encyclical letters of the Pope, statements from *synods* (meetings of some bishops with the Pope), and individual instruction from bishops to the faithful in their dioceses.

Although the bishops, taken individually, do not enjoy the privilege of infallibility, they do, however, proclaim infallibly the doctrine of Christ. . . .

When, even though dispersed throughout the world but preserving for all that amongst themselves and with Peter's successor the bond of communion, in their authoritative teaching concerning matters of faith and morals, they are in agreement that a particular teaching is to be held definitively and absolutely (LG, 25).

The Church Governs

In our consideration of the Church's authority so far we have been concerned with matters of *doctrine*. Doctrines of our faith are those elements that are the essential beliefs of our faith. The creeds contain many of these doctrines. But the authority of the Church is not limited to matters of doctrine, on faith and morals. The Church also has authority to govern her members. This authority is exercised in matters of *discipline*. The Church, like any society, has the right and the need to formulate

"... If I ask anyone: 'Would you rather have your joy in truth or in falsehood?' he would say: 'In truth', with just as little hesitation as he would say that he wants to be happy. And certainly the happy life is joy in truth, which means joy in you, who are truth, God, *my light, health of my countenance, my God*."

(St. Augustine, *Confessions*, bk. X, chap. 23)

rules for her members for their own good, to lead them to holiness of life. These rules do not pertain to our beliefs but to our actions.

If we look at some of our Church disciplines we can see how the Church governs us. For example, the Church tells us that we may not eat meat on Ash Wednesday or the Fridays of Lent. This is a matter of discipline and not part of our creed. But we follow this rule because we believe that the Church should direct us in such matters for our spiritual good. Another example is the Church law that requires us to *fast* (abstain from eating), except for good reason, for one hour before receiving Holy Communion. Other examples of the Church's authority to govern are the obligation to participate in Mass on certain Holy Days and the rules concerning certain liturgical rites. Can you think of others? Each of these laws is a legitimate use of the Church's governing power to ensure that Christ's Church and her members will remain strong.

One further point should be made about the distinction between matters of discipline and matters of doctrine. Matters of doctrine are those things in our faith that have been revealed to us by God and thus cannot be changed by us. They cannot even be changed by those in authority in the Church. But matters of discipline are those practices that have developed over time, laws made by the proper authorities, and thus they can be changed by them. This has happened in the past and may well happen again.

Obedience

We, as faithful Catholics, have an obligation to respond properly to the Church's authority. We have an obligation to believe the doctrines of the faith if we wish to be members of the Church. We will never completely understand the great mysteries of our faith. They are rich in meaning and above us, and we must strive to learn more about them, to love them, to study them, and to exercise the virtue of faith.

In matters of discipline we must be *obedient*. Obedience means that we should comply with the will of another who has the authority to command us. We have already seen that the Church has such authority from Christ. Remember that the Church speaks for Christ; the obedience and respect that we show to Christ's representatives are the same obedience and respect we would show to Christ himself.

There may be times when a particular Church law seems unclear or unwise to us. What do we do then? The following analogy will help you understand. The quarterback on a football team is in a position of authority, and the rest of the team must listen to him and obey him when he calls the play. In fact, they trust him to make his calls wisely. While they must understand the calls, it is not necessary that they understand why he calls a particular play at a certain time. The other players try to understand why a call is made, but if they cannot they assume that the quarterback knows what he is doing. In order to win the game they must follow his directions.

The faithful in the Church must act like the players on the football team. We should strive to understand the spirit that animates the law and then obey it. If we cannot understand it right away, we must presume that those in authority do. This is not blind obedience, for we have first tried to understand and then submitted ourselves to those who do. We should try to understand the Church's laws and to obey them in a spirit of charity. The authority of the Church comes from Christ, who told his apostles that his power was being given to them.

Words to Know:

Pope	bishop	hierarchy
ex cathedra	impeccability	synod
infallibility	magisterium	primacy

Q. 14 *Who is the Pope?*

The Pope is the successor of St. Peter in the See of Rome, and in the primacy, namely in the universal apostolate and episcopal power. Therefore he is the visible head of the entire Church, the Vicar of Jesus Christ, who is the invisible head; hence this Church is called the Roman Catholic Church.

Q. 15 *What do the Pope and the bishops united with him constitute?*

The Pope and the bishops united with him constitute the teaching Church, that is, the one that has received from Jesus Christ the mission of teaching the truths and laws of God to all men. And men receive only from this teaching Church the full and secure knowledge that is necessary to live in a Christian manner.

Q. 16 *Can the teaching Church err in teaching the truths revealed by God?*

The teaching Church cannot err in teaching the truths revealed by God: she is infallible, because ''the Spirit of truth'' (Jn 15:26), as promised by Jesus Christ, assists her continually.

Q. 17 *Can the Pope, taken separately, err in truths revealed by God?*

The Pope, taken separately, cannot err in teaching the truths revealed by God; that is, he is infallible, just as the Church is, when, as pastor and teacher of all Christians, he defines doctrine on faith and morals.

Prayer

''Almighty and eternal God, you guide all things by your word, you govern all Christian people. In your love protect the Pope you have chosen for us. Under his leadership deepen our faith and make us better Christians. We ask this through Christ our Lord. *Amen.*''

(General Intercessions for Holy Week)

CHAPTER 6

The Visible Hierarchical Church

"You are Peter, the rock, and upon this rock I will build my Church" *(Mt 16:18).*

We have seen that Christ founded his Church and willed her basic structure. He built her on Peter. Our Lord himself gave us the outlines of the Church's hierarchy. As is mentioned numerous times in the Gospels, Christ chose twelve apostles, and he gave them the power to carry on his work—teaching, governing, and through the sacraments sanctifying the faithful. He said to the apostles,

Whatever you bind on earth will be bound in Heaven; whatever you loose on earth will be loosed in Heaven (Mt 16:19).

Successors to the Apostles

Christ gave the apostles the mission of evangelizing all nations. Since *all* nations could evidently not be evangelized by the apostles during their lifetime, Jesus was of course addressing all those who would be their successors down through the centuries.

The apostles also understood him in this way, because immediately after the Ascension, as recorded in the Acts of the Apostles (1:15–26), Peter stood up and told the disciples that he and they must choose someone to replace Judas. They chose Matthias. Thus they began to exercise their power to bind and loose by electing the first successor to an apostle.

Christ in his wisdom chose this structure. He knew that the Church, like any society, would need authority to govern. Without it the Church would be in chaos. In the Old Testament we also see a certain amount of structure among the chosen people. There were different tribes with clearly defined territories, and, sometimes, special functions. For instance, priests came only from the tribe of Levi. There were leaders chosen not by men but by God, such as Abraham, Moses, and David. In the New Testament, which is the fulfillment of the Old, we see the establishment of a hierarchical Church, with divine authority. It is important to realize that the Church is not a federal union or democracy where majority opinion prevails, a corporation where managerial skills are uppermost, or an organization where efficiency is first. The Church may use human wisdom, but she is far above human wisdom. She is supernatural in her essential structure. God says, "As the heavens are higher than the earth, so are my ways higher than your ways and my thoughts than your thoughts" (Is 55:9).

As we have see this hierarchical Church

started to function at the very outset, after Christ's Ascension.

Later in the Acts we find the account of the Council of Jerusalem (Acts 15). At this council several of the apostles and other leaders of the early Church met to solve certain questions concerning the gentile members of the Church. Both of these incidents show us that the apostles understood Our Lord's command for them to build up the Church.

The apostles received from Christ the fullness of his powers which they, in turn, passed on to the bishops, their successors. In the early Church each bishop was responsible for the Christians in a particular area. As the Church grew, the apostles passed on their power to other men, increasing the number of bishops. It is this same power that the bishops today have received, making them the successors of the apostles.

Church Structure

Today the Church is spread throughout the world and is divided into various *dioceses*. At the head of each diocese is a bishop, whose role is to teach, govern, and sanctify the faithful in his care. Some bishops have received the title of *archbishop*. An archbishop is the head of an important diocese—usually the oldest in a particular area. His diocese is then called an *archdiocese*. The archbishop has the same power and responsibility as a bishop. All of the bishops are united under the bishop of Rome— the Pope, who is the Vicar of Christ on earth. Just as Peter had authority over the other apostles, the bishop of Rome has the authority to lead the other bishops and to teach the entire Church.

As the Church continued to grow in the early days, other men—deacons and priests —were appointed and given a share in his powers by the bishop. This is still true today. Because the bishop cannot personally care for all the people within his diocese, the territory is further divided into *parishes*. The bishop then delegates his authority and the power to celebrate some of the sacraments to the *priests* in charge of these parishes. Each parish is headed by a *pastor*, who usually has one or more assistants to help him care for the spiritual needs of the parishioners. As a pastor (which comes from the Latin word for shepherd), he is to lead and serve the flock entrusted to his care. The pastor's work is one of service. Christ asked the shepherds to give their very lives for those in their care. Like the bishops, priests share in the priesthood of Christ, principally by celebrating Mass and forgiving sins. They do not, however, have the power of the bishop to ordain others to the priesthood. The priest also shares in the teaching office of the bishop when he preaches at Mass or instructs the faithful of his parish.

There are also *deacons*, whose role is to assist the bishop. They, like priests, are usually assigned by the bishop to work in a parish and help in the care of the faithful. The deacon is ordained by the bishop but does not have the power to say Mass. He can administer the sacrament of Baptism and witness marriages for the Church. He also shares in the teaching office of the bishop through his preaching. The deacon may also help the priest by visiting the sick, counseling the bereaved, or practicing other works of mercy in the diocese.

Some priests and bishops are made cardinals with the job of electing the Pope and being his closest advisors. Some priests are given the honorary title monsignor. These two groups are not steps within the sacrament of Holy Orders as the others are. Monsignor is an honorary title given by the Pope to many priests. The office of cardinal is also an honor bestowed by the Pope. At the present time most cardinals are chosen from among the bishops of the Church, although at other times in history some were priests or even laymen. The primary function of the cardinals is to elect the Pope, who has for many centuries been elected from among the *college of cardinals*.

In addition to this, the cardinals assist the Pope in the *curia*. The curia consists of the many administrative and judicial offices by which the Pope directs the Church. We might think of it as similar, in some ways, to the President of the United States and his various cabinet offices. Each of the curial offices is usually headed by one of the cardinals, although some may be headed by a bishop or priest.

Not all of these offices in the Church are essential. Since the bishops have the fullness of Christ's priesthood, they can provide for all of our spiritual needs. Without the bishops we would not have the sacramental life, which Our Lord gave us for our salvation. This simple structure may have been enough for the early Church. However, now that the Church has grown so large, those who assist the bishops—priests and deacons—make it possible for many more people to receive the graces of Christ.

Just as the authority of the Church comes from Christ, so Christ gave to his Church the power to sanctify. In the next chapter we will look at those sacraments that both sanctify us and incorporate us into the Church.

Words to Know:

diocese   monsignor
cardinal   curia

Q. 18 *Who are the legitimate pastors of the Church?*
The legitimate pastors of the Church are the Pope, the Supreme Pontiff, and the bishops united with him.

CHAPTER 7

The Church Sanctifying: Sacraments of Membership

"And the Word was made flesh and dwelt among us, full of grace and truth; we have beheld his glory, glory as of the only Son of the Father. And from his fullness have we all received, grace upon grace" (Jn 1:14, 16).

To help us understand the Church's role in the dispensation of grace let us consider for a moment the parable of the Good Samaritan. You may already be familiar with this parable, but today we will look at it in a slightly different light.

A man was going down from Jerusalem to Jericho, and he fell among robbers, who stripped him and beat him and departed, leaving him half dead. Now by chance a priest was going down that road; and when he saw him he passed by on the other side. So likewise a Levite, when he came to the place and saw him, passed by on the other side. But a Samaritan, as he journeyed, came to where he was; and when he saw him, he had compassion, and went to him and bound up his wounds, pouring on oil and wine; then he set him on his own beast and brought him to an inn, and took care of him. And the next day

he took out two denarii and gave them to the innkeeper, saying, "Take care of him; whatever you spend, I will repay you when I come back" (Luke 10:30−35).

We know that Our Lord told this parable in answer to a question about who is our neighbor. This parable teaches us a lesson about real charity. However, it seems that Our Lord also had a deeper message in mind about grace and the sacraments. As the fourth-century bishop St. Augustine explained in one of his sermons, this parable teaches us about our salvation.

Let us suppose that the man who is traveling from Jerusalem to Jericho is Adam, who also represents the whole human race. He was "robbed"—by the devil—of his riches, that is, the life of grace. Just as the man was left half-dead by the side of the road, the human race is weak, fallen, and without the many gifts God intended for us. Most important, after the Fall we were unable to attain salvation. The priest and the Levite signify the priests and the prophets of the Old Covenant, who were unable to restore us to supernatural life. Finally, the Samaritan pouring oil and wine on the man's wounds represents Christ, who "pours out" graces through the sacraments to heal our spiritual wounds.

Discussion Question: Based on St. Augustine's explanation of this parable, explain the significance of the "inn" and the "innkeeper". What other symbols (relating to this theme of grace) can you find in this parable?

Sacraments of Initiation

The main purpose of all the sacraments is to give us grace and bring us to salvation. However, three of these sacraments are also important to our life as members of the Church. In fact, Baptism, Holy Eucharist, and Confirmation are the sacraments by which we are fully incorporated into the Body of Christ. These sacraments are sometimes called *sacraments of initiation*, since they bring us into the Church and give us full participation in her. They also signify our unity in the Body of Christ.

Baptism

Baptism is the sacrament that frees us from original sin and fills us with divine life—sanctifying grace. We receive the Holy Spirit, who then lives in us. It makes us children of God and heirs to the Kingdom of Heaven. This sacrament unites us with Christ in a special way, giving us an invisible seal, or mark, which can never be taken away.

Yet the effect of Baptism goes far beyond our own personal lives. Baptism makes us members of the Mystical Body of Christ. In St. Paul's letter to the Corinthians he tells us, "For by one Spirit we were all baptized into one body . . . and all were made to drink of the one Spirit" (1 Cor 12:13). So Baptism makes us members of the Church and unites us closely with all those who have been baptized in Christ.

Baptism is also the gateway to all the other sacraments. Once we have become part of the Church we are able to receive from her the graces dispensed through the other sacraments.

The Eucharist

The next sacrament we will discuss is the Eucharist, which in itself is the most important of the sacraments. First of all, it is a

"I tell you solemnly, if you do not eat the Flesh of the Son of Man and drink his Blood, you will not have life in you."

(Jn 6:53)

source of spiritual food. This aspect of the Eucharist was prefigured in many ways in the Old Testament—for example, when the manna in the desert nourished the Israelites for many years. In the New Testament, after the multiplication of the loaves and the fishes, Our Lord spoke to his disciples about the "Bread of Life":

> Jesus said to them, "I am the Bread of Life; he who comes to me shall not hunger, and he who believes in me shall never thirst. . . . Your fathers ate manna in the wilderness, and they died. This is the Bread which comes down from Heaven, that a man may eat of it and not die. I am the living Bread which comes down from Heaven; if any one eats of this Bread, he will live for ever; and the Bread which I shall give for the life of the world is my Flesh. . . . Truly, truly, I say to you, unless you eat of the Flesh of the Son of Man and drink his Blood, you have no life in you; he who eats my Flesh and drinks my Blood has eternal life, and I will raise him up on the last day" (Jn 6:35, 49−51, 53−54).

Our Lord tells us here of the necessity to nourish the life of grace born in us through Baptism. Just as our bodies require nourishment, we must "feed" the life of grace through reception of the Eucharist, the *Flesh* and *Blood* of which Our Lord speaks.

Furthermore, the sacrament of the Eucharist is both a cause and a sign of the unity of the Church. The Eucharist causes first our union with Christ and through him our union with one another. All those who receive Christ are truly united through this sacrament. St. Paul affirms this also, in his letter to the Corinthians, when he says, "Because there is one Bread, we who are many are one body, for we all partake of the one Bread" (1 Cor 10:17). It is this union with Christ and his Body that is signified by the words *Holy Communion*.

Even the elements of bread and wine chosen by Our Lord for this sacrament signify the very unity that it brings about. Just as many grains of wheat make up the one loaf of bread, and many grapes produce the one cup of wine, so too many Christians are joined into the one Body of Christ through the Eucharist.

Confirmation

The third sacrament of initiation is Confirmation. Confirmation is the sacrament in which we receive the fullness of the Holy Spirit. This enables us to profess our faith as strong and perfect Christians and soldiers of Jesus Christ.

Although we receive the Holy Spirit at Baptism, Confirmation completes what is begun in Baptism and has been nourished through the Eucharist. The new life of grace that we receive, usually as infants, is strengthened in us at Confirmation. At Baptism we were spiritual infants in the Church; at Confirmation we become spiritual adults.

We know from our experience that, as we grow older, we take on more and more responsibilities. When you become an adult, you will have to bear the responsibilities of citizenship

—voting, paying taxes, and perhaps fighting to defend your country.

The same is true in the Church. As adult Christians we have the responsibility to bear witness to Christ. This means that we must live for Christ in our daily lives, defend Christ and our faith when it is challenged, and perhaps even die as *martyrs*. The graces of Confirmation prepare us to meet these challenges.

The notion of defending our faith has led many of the Church Fathers to speak of Confirmation making us *soldiers of Christ*. St. Paul uses this idea when he writes to the Christians in Ephesus, encouraging them to be strong in their faith:

> Therefore take the whole armor of God, that you may be able to withstand in the evil day, and having done all, to stand. Stand therefore, having girded your loins with truth and having put on the breastplate of righteousness; . . . above all, taking the shield of faith with which you can quench all the flaming darts of the evil one. And take the helmet of salvation, and the sword of the Spirit, which is the word of God (Eph 6:13−14, 16−17).

We must pray then that we use the gift of the Holy Spirit to strengthen and defend our faith always.

As members of the Mystical Body united through these sacraments we have obligations to live as part of Christ's Church. We must accept the teachings of the Church and follow the laws that she has wisely set down.

We must also continuously strengthen our faith through reading and instruction. We know that Confirmation is usually preceded by an intense period of instruction preparing us for our place as adult Christians. However, growth in knowledge and understanding of our faith should not end here. Just as most of us continue our secular education in an informal way after completing school, we must continue our education in our faith. We must strive to deepen our understanding so that we may draw closer to God and our eternal goal.

Rites in the Church

With these three sacraments comes full membership in the Church. But the way the sacraments are celebrated may vary. This is because the Catholic Church is composed of various *rites*. Here a rite refers to a common way of worship and of practicing the faith by a particular group of Catholics.

These rites are ancient in origin, and all of them can be traced back, in some way, to the days of the apostles. When the apostles set out to "teach all nations", they had received the Holy Spirit and were well-grounded in the doctrines of the faith. But they had not yet settled on the precise forms for the various ceremonies. In fact, these ceremonies developed over a long period of time and reflected the cultures, languages, and history of the various places where the gospel was preached.

As the Church grew, each bishop celebrated Mass and administered the sacraments according to the customs of the city where he lived. Certain cities eventually exercised more influence than others on the surrounding countryside. Of course, Rome, as the center of both the Roman Empire and the Church itself, was the most important. Constantinople (modern-day Istanbul in Turkey) was the center of the eastern half of the empire and became quite important too.

In the Church today there are several different rites. The largest of these—and the one with which you are probably most familiar—is the *Roman rite*, which is used throughout the Western world. It is called "Roman" because the ceremonies originally come from the diocese of Rome. The second-largest rite is the *Byzantine rite*. This rite comes from the ceremonies of the church in the city of Byzantium, or Constantinople—the eastern part of the old Roman Empire. There are also several smaller rites whose origins can be found in other Eastern parts of the world.

These rites are all united under Christ and his Vicar on earth—the Pope. All who belong to them are members of the Catholic Church. The fundamental beliefs are the same, but the expression of those beliefs and the ceremonies vary according to the different cultural origins. To help you understand, let us look at a few differences between the Roman rite and the Byzantine rite.

In the Roman rite, *unleavened* bread is used for the Eucharist, while Byzantine Catholics use *leavened* bread. While Roman-rite Catholics traditionally genuflect before the Blessed Sacrament, Byzantine-rite Catholics have always bowed as a sign of respect. Members of the Roman rite make the Sign of the Cross from left to right; members of the Byzantine rite do so from right to left. The churches of the Byzantine rite are decorated with *icons*, flat paintings of Our Lord, Our Lady, or the saints, often done on wood and decorated with gold and jewels. The churches of the Roman rite often contain statues in addition to other kinds of images. You will not usually find statues in a Byzantine church.

As you can see, the differences are not in essential beliefs. Both reverence the Eucharist as the Body and Blood of Christ, even though respect is shown to this great sacrament in different ways. This variety enriches the Church, but it also points back to its unity, since all are part of *one* Church.

We have seen that it is through her sacramental life that the Church sanctifies her members. In the next chapter we will consider the form of the Church's worship.

Words to Know:

rite   icon   sacraments of initiation

Church Teaching

"The Holy Catholic Church, which is the Mystical Body of Christ, is made up of the faithful who are organically united in the Holy Spirit by the same faith, the same sacraments and the same government. They combine into different groups, which are held together by their hierarchy, and so form particular churches or rites. Between those churches there is such a wonderful bond of union that this variety in the Universal Church, so far from diminishing its unity, rather serves to emphasize it. For the Catholic Church wishes the traditions of each particular church or rite to remain whole and entire, and it likewise wishes to adapt its own way of life to the needs of different times and places" (OE, 2).

CHAPTER 8

The Church Sanctifying: Worship

"The Liturgy is the summit toward which the activity of the Church is directed; it is also the fount from which all her power flows" (SC, 4).

Men have worshipped their Creator since the beginning of the world. Long before Christianity, many civilizations had elaborate forms of public worship that had been established for centuries. These pagan peoples recognized the need to offer something to their Creator in return for the many benefits that they had received. They also recognized that this worship should be public, since so many of their blessings were received in common. The great civilization of Greece, which rose to prominence in the centuries immediately preceding the coming of Christ, was one that practiced public worship.

The word "liturgy" comes from the Greek and means "public work". Originally, this referred to any public act, especially those done by the wealthy for the benefit of the rest of society. It was understood that people who had benefited were bound to make some return from these benefits. Thus they would often sponsor plays or some other work for the whole society. By extension, the word was transferred to acts of worship, since the wealthy would often support these as well. As we will use the word here, liturgy means the Church's official public worship. This worship of God must be performed both as individuals and as a people. The Liturgy differs from our private devotions and prayers in being public and in having an external and a formal aspect. It is the action of Christ and his entire Church, rather than the action of an individual. Christ said, "Where two or three are gathered together in my name, there I am in the midst of them" (Mt 18:20).

Through the Liturgy we, the Mystical Body of Christ, are united with Christ in his priestly role to give honor and praise to God. It is proper that the Church as a whole people should do this, since the Church as a whole people was given the graces necessary for salvation. The Liturgy allows us as a whole people to offer to God the highest praise possible, since in it we unite ourselves with Christ in praising the Father. It also adds a new dimension to prayer, since we join in the heavenly chorus of the Communion of Saints, who all belong to the Church. Praying in community lifts up our hearts and increases charity.

Three elements make up the Liturgy: (1) the

Eucharist, that is, the Holy Sacrifice of the Mass, (2) the sacraments, and (3) the Divine Office, or Liturgy of the Hours. Each time the Mass is offered, the perfect sacrifice of Calvary, that is, the whole Paschal mystery, the Passion, death, and Resurrection of Christ, is renewed on our altars. The Mass, then, is the most important element, since it is here that we join most perfectly with Christ offering himself to the Father. We can take part in the Mass most perfectly by worthily receiving the Body and Blood of Christ in the sacrament of the Eucharist.

The remaining six sacraments make up the second element of the Liturgy. These are the special channels of God's grace, given to us by Jesus Christ and enabling us to participate in the supernatural life. Over the centuries the prayers and ceremonies that accompany the sacraments have changed, but the essential form was established by Christ himself.

Finally, the public worship of the Church is carried out by the daily recitation of the Divine Office, or Liturgy of the Hours. The Liturgy of the Hours is a prayer of praise composed of Psalms, prayers, instructions, and readings from Scripture and the writings of the saints. These are divided into segments called "hours", each of which is to be prayed at certain times during the day. This enables us to sanctify the entire day by praising God. Priests and other religious have a special obligation to recite, say, or sing the Office, but it is prayed by many lay people as well.

In order that the Liturgy may truly be a sign of the unity of the Church, the Church has laid down certain fixed and universal rules for its proper celebration. In this way, Catholics all over the world can join together in one act of public worship. These rituals also ensure that the Liturgy is reverent, dignified, and worthy of being offered to God.

The Liturgical Year

Our natural lives are governed to a great extent by the natural rhythm of the seasons. As the year passes, our lives are affected by the seasons in nature. As we pass from one season to another, we must change our clothing, our activities, and even the food we eat. We also notice that the colors in nature change as we move from one season to another, for example, the changing colors of the leaves in autumn. The life of the Church is similar to this pattern in nature. The Church year is divided into seasons as well. As we move from one season to another, our spiritual lives and activities change, just as our natural lives and activities change with the passing of the seasons. As in nature we see the colors change with the seasons, so too, in the Church's year we see a change in colors. This Church year is known as the liturgical year. Each division, or season, of the year has its own special prayers for the Mass and the Divine Office. The mysteries of God are so great and inexhaustible that we will always have to continue to grow in understanding and love. Since we are unable to grasp Christ's revelation all at once, our Mother the Church shows us one facet at a time rhythmically during the whole liturgical year. The person of Jesus has so many varied aspects—such as mercy, gentleness, majesty, justice, authority, tenderness, severity, compassion, sorrow, serenity, love, peace, and many more—that we will never come to the end of the mystery that is Jesus, and thus never finish praising him.

The liturgical year is based upon the three major feasts of Christmas, Easter, and Pentecost. (See the diagram on page 46.) These feasts celebrate the principal events in the history of our salvation: the Incarnation, that is, the second Person of the Trinity becoming man; the Redemption, that is, the suffering, death, and Resurrection of Our Lord; and Pentecost, that is, the descent of the Holy Spirit upon the apostles, which is the birthday of the Church. Of these three feasts, Christmas and Easter are especially important, and thus they require periods of preparation as well as periods of celebration. Easter is the most important, and therefore the periods of preparation and celebration are longer. Let us now look at the seasons of the liturgical year.

Advent and Christmas

The liturgical year begins on a Sunday in late November or early December, four weeks before Christmas, with the season of Advent. Advent is the penitential season of preparation that precedes the feast of Christmas. The word *Advent* comes from the Latin word that means ''coming''.

During Advent the Church meditates on both past and future events. In the centuries before Christ, God's chosen people awaited and kept themselves prepared for the birth of a Savior. Likewise, we prepare ourselves to celebrate Christmas, the feast of his first ''coming'' among us. During this period, we also contemplate the *second* coming of Christ at the end of the world. The Liturgy of Advent prepares us for this event as well.

Advent is a season of penance, since this is the best way to prepare our hearts for Christ. The readings and prayers in the Mass and the Divine Office focus upon this idea and help us to meditate on the two comings of Christ. We hear in the Gospel, for example, the message of John the Baptist about repenting in order to prepare for the Messiah's coming. We also hear the words of Isaiah on a similar theme.

Despite this penitential theme, Advent retains a sense of joyful expectation, since the coming of the Savior is an event of great joy. We should rejoice, since the Savior was in fact born among us. On the third of the four Sundays of Advent, the Church particularly reminds us of this through the liturgical readings and prayers. This Sunday is called ''Gaudete Sunday'', taken from the Latin word meaning ''rejoice''.

The season of Advent ends with the midnight Mass on December 24, as the Church begins her celebration of the great feast of Christmas. This feast celebrates the nativity of our Savior and is the beginning of the Christmas season. In contrast to Advent, this is a season of great joy. It includes the feast of the Epiphany, when we celebrate the revelation of Christ to the Gentiles, represented by the three wise men, and it ends with the feast of the Baptism of Christ.

Lent and Easter

The next season of the year is the season of preparation for the feast of Easter. It is called Lent and begins on Ash Wednesday. The ashes we receive on that day remind us of our own mortality. The Lenten season lasts for forty days, a little more than six weeks. The forty days represent the forty days Jesus spent in the desert preparing for his public life. In the Liturgy of Lent the Church urges us, through the readings and prayers, to do penance in reparation for our sins. We can do this through fasting, self-denial, almsgiving, and other good works.

Since this season is so closely linked to the suffering and death of Our Lord, the Liturgy does not express the sense of expectant joy that permeated the Advent season. Nevertheless, the Church does set aside the fourth Sunday in Lent to express our anticipated joy in Christ's Resurrection. This Sunday is called "Laetare Sunday", taken from another Latin word, meaning "rejoice".

The final week of Lent, Holy Week, is particularly important. During this week we concentrate on the events leading up to the Crucifixion of Our Lord. The Gospels that record the Passion of Christ are solemnly read, and the other prayers and readings directly focus on these events.

The season of Lent ends with the solemn announcement of the Resurrection of Our Lord Jesus Christ at the Easter Vigil Mass on Holy Saturday evening. At this Mass we begin our celebration of the feast of Easter and the Easter season. The Easter season is marked by a sense of triumphant joy, since Jesus has overcome death and risen from the dead. This season lasts for fifty days, concluding with the third major feast of the liturgical year, the feast of Pentecost.

Pentecost

Pentecost is the feast that celebrates the presence of the Holy Spirit in the Church. Just as the Holy Spirit spoke through the prophets in the Old Testament, Our Lord promised to his apostles at the Last Supper that he would send the Holy Spirit to guide his Church. ". . . the Holy Spirit . . . will teach you all things and bring to your remembrance all that I have said to you" (Jn 14:26). This promise was fulfilled on the first Pentecost, and our celebration of this feast reminds us of this great gift.

Prayer

"It is truly right that with full hearts and minds and voices we should praise the unseen God, the all-powerful Father, and his only Son, Our Lord Jesus Christ."

(Easter proclamation: *Exsultet*)

Ordinary Time

There remains the time in the liturgical year that falls between Christmas and Lent and between Easter and Advent. This time is called ordinary time, since it is not marked by one of the principal events of our faith. "Ordinary", however, does not mean unimportant. This time allows us to reflect more deeply on the mysteries that we have just celebrated and to develop our love for God more fully. Certain Sundays and Holy Days during this time are also set aside to commemorate other significant elements of our faith or events from the life of Our Lord and Our Lady.

The diagram that follows will help us to see these seasons of the year more clearly.

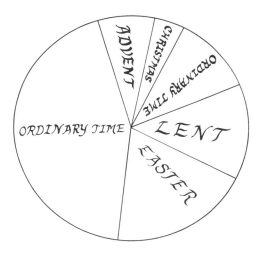

Other Feasts

Now that we have seen the basic framework for the liturgical year, we will fill it in with some of the feasts that occur throughout the year. We can divide these into three main groups: (1) Holy Days, (2) Sunday feasts, and (3) feasts of the saints and Our Blessed Mother. The Church has set aside several days out of the year to commemorate certain significant events in our faith. In the United States,

six of these feasts are Holy Days of Obligation, that is, days on which we are obliged to attend Mass. They are: (1) the Immaculate Conception of Our Lady (December 8); (2) Christmas (December 25); (3) the Solemnity of Mary, the Mother of God (January 1); (4) Ascension Thursday (forty days after Easter); (5) the Assumption of Our Lady (August 15); and (6) All Saints' Day (November 1). As you can see, these feasts occur throughout the liturgical year, except for during the season of Lent.

Several great feasts of the Church are celebrated on Sundays throughout the year. Like the Holy Days, these special Sundays are found throughout the liturgical seasons. During the Christmas season we celebrate the *Feast of the Holy Family*, the model for all families, on the Sunday after Christmas. In the United States the *Feast of the Epiphany* is celebrated on the Sunday closest to January 6. On the following Sunday we celebrate the *Baptism of Jesus*, which marked the beginning of his public life.

In the ordinary time after Pentecost we celebrate two other great mysteries of our faith: the Trinity (on *Trinity Sunday*) and the Eucharist (on the *Feast of Corpus Christi*). Finally, the liturgical year ends with the *Feast of Christ the King*, which reminds us to look ahead to the time when Christ will come in glory and reign as our King.

In addition to Sundays and Holy Days, there are many weekdays throughout the liturgical year that are set aside as special commemorations. Several recall events from the life of Our Blessed Mother. Others honor the saints as great examples of the Christian life. On these days we should call upon Mary and the saints to pray to God on our behalf.

Return to the diagram to see how the feasts fit into the liturgical year. As you have already seen, the colors of the liturgical year change. We see this most clearly in the vestments—the special garments worn by the priest and other ministers for celebrating the Liturgy—but also in other decorations in our churches. The three major colors are purple, white, and green. These are used at particular times during the various seasons of the year. *Purple* symbolizes penance and sorrow, so it is used during the seasons of Advent and Lent. *White* symbolizes joy and glory, so it is used at Christmas and Easter. *Green* symbolizes life and hope, so it is used during the ordinary time, when we should be filled with hope.

Three other colors are used less frequently, but also serve to remind us of what we are celebrating. First among these is *red*, which symbolizes fire and blood. It is used on the feast of Pentecost for the Holy Spirit, who was symbolized by fire. It is also used when we celebrate the Passion of Our Lord, the feasts of the martyrs, the feasts of apostles, and the feasts of the evangelists. *Rose* is symbolic of joy in the midst of penance and is used on Laetare and Gaudete Sundays. As we have seen, these Sundays occur during the penitential seasons and are days of rejoicing. Finally, the color *black* is a symbol of mourning. It may be used for Masses for the dead or All Souls' Day.

Thus, we have seen how the Church provides us with a beautiful and meaningful way of worshipping God throughout the year. It enables us to reflect on the key mysteries of our faith and the lives of Our Lord and his Mother as we go from season to season. In order to unite ourselves more perfectly with our fellow Christians, our prayers should reflect the themes so beautifully set forth for us by the Church. Thus, our entire prayer life will become a more perfect form of worship to be given to Almighty God.

Words to Know:

Liturgy   vestment   liturgical year

Church Teaching

"The sacred liturgy is the public worship which Our Redeemer as Head of the Church renders to the Father, as well as the worship which the community of the faithful renders to its Founder and through him to the Heavenly Father. It is, in short, the worship rendered by the Mystical Body of Christ in the entirety of its head and members" (MD).

CHAPTER 9

Mary—Mother of the Church

". . . the angel Gabriel was sent from God to a city of Galilee named Nazareth, to a virgin . . . and the virgin's name was Mary. And he came to her and said, 'Hail, full of grace, the Lord is with you! . . . Do not be afraid, Mary, for you have found favor with God. And behold, you will conceive and bear a son, and you shall call his name Jesus. . . .' And Mary said, 'Behold, I am the handmaid of the Lord; let it be done to me according to your word.' And the angel departed from her" (Lk 1:26−28, 30−31, 38).

These words from St. Luke describe the *Annunciation* and mark the first reference in the Gospels to Mary, the mother of Our Lord. It is appropriate that we should first see her in this scene, since our salvation depends in a great way on this event. Mary was not forced to become the Mother of God. God announced to her through his messenger Gabriel that she had been chosen for this role. Yet his choice required her consent. This consent is beautifully and simply given by Our Lady in her words, "Let it be done to me according to your word."

At the moment of Mary's *fiat* (the Latin word for "let it be done") the "Word became flesh". In other words, the Son of God was conceived in her womb. Mary freely accepted God's will for her and gave life to the Son of God so that we might share in his divine life. Thus, our very salvation depended upon Mary's obedience to the will of God.

The New Eve

Mary's importance for our redemption is reflected in the title frequently given to her by the Fathers of the Church—the "new Eve". Christ has been called the "new Adam", because by his death he undid the harm done by Adam, the first man. So, too, we can speak of Mary and compare her to Eve. "Eve" means "the mother of all the living". Eve helped to bring sin into the world by tempting Adam. Mary, however, helped to bring salvation from sin by listening to and accepting the invitation of God and then becoming the Mother of God. Eve brought death into the world, but Mary brought life—eternal life through Christ. Mary's faith and obedience to God's will correct Eve's pride and disobedience of God's command. Mary, by submitting herself perfectly to God's will, returned to mankind what had been lost to us through original sin.

Mary, Our Mother

As Eve was the physical mother of the human race, Mary is our spiritual Mother.

While hanging on the Cross, Our Lord spoke to Mary and the apostle John. He said to Mary, "Woman, behold your son!" And then he turned to John and said, "Behold, your Mother!" (Jn 19:26–27). These words were meant not only for Our Lady and St. John, but for all of Jesus' followers. Jesus gave his own Mother to all of us. When Jesus said he would not leave us orphans, he also meant to leave us his Mother. Her care for us is evident in many ways. We call Mary *"Our Blessed Mother"*. Like any mother, Mary has a special love for every one of her children. She leads us into her Son's presence. She watches over each and shares in each one's joys and sorrows. In turning to Mary, as we would to our own mother on earth, we draw closer to God.

In addition to being a spiritual Mother to each of us as individuals, Mary is also the Mother of the whole Church. As Mary was the Mother of Christ's physical body, she is also the Mother of his Mystical Body—the Church—of which we are members through our Baptism.

Mary's role in our redemption goes beyond giving birth to Christ. Her cooperation in God's will began at the Annunciation and continued to the foot of the Cross. There, Mary willingly accepted the death of her Son and joined with him in that suffering. The graces that Christ won for us come to us through Mary. It is for this reason that we can say, "to Jesus, through Mary".

Privileges Given to Mary

Because Mary was chosen by God to be the Mother of his divine Son, he gave to

Prayer

"Mary, Mother of Grace, Mother of Mercy, shield me from the enemy and receive me at the hour of my death."

(*Enchiridion*, 61)

49

her several *privileges*. Three of these are: (1) freedom from original sin, (2) complete and perpetual virginity, and (3) freedom from having body and soul separated until the end of the world.

Free from Original Sin

We know that all human beings have inherited original sin from our first parents, Adam and Eve. When they sinned, they lost for themselves—and for us—the great gift of *sanctifying grace*, God's life in our souls. While we are not personally responsible for original sin, we bear the effects—especially being weak and easily tempted to sin.

Because God wished Mary to be worthy to become the Mother of God, she was created free from all sin. God prepared Mary so that she would be worthy to carry the Son of God in her womb. In the same way, the ark of the Covenant was built in the Old Testament to be a fitting receptacle for the written Word of God. God instructed the people, through Moses, that the ark should be built of a rare wood and elaborately decorated with gold. In this way it would be an appropriate symbol of God's presence. How much more fitting was it, then, that God should prepare Mary, who would contain the Word of God himself, not just a symbol of God's presence. Mary is, then, the "new Ark of the Covenant".

Besides Our Lord, Mary is the only human being who was created without original sin. As the poet Wordsworth so beautifully put it, she is "our tainted nature's solitary boast". From the moment of her conception in the womb of her mother, St. Anne, Mary was filled with divine life. Because she was without original sin, she was free from our weakness and inclination to sin. She truly was, as the archangel Gabriel said, "full of grace". This great privilege is called the *Immaculate Conception*.

This doctrine has been taught by the Church but was not formally defined until December 8, 1854, by Pope Pius IX. This was an occasion when papal infallibility was invoked. Our Lady herself confirmed this doctrine four years later. When she appeared to St. Bernadette in the grotto at Lourdes, she identified herself by this title. When asked who she was, Mary replied, "I am the Immaculate Conception."

The feast of the Immaculate Conception, celebrated on December 8, has become a Holy Day of Obligation since the doctrine was defined. This feast is particularly important for Catholics in the United States, for it is under this title that Mary was declared patroness of our country.

Perpetual Virginity

A second great privilege given to Mary was that of *perpetual virginity*. This doctrine means that Mary was always a virgin: before the conception and birth of Christ, during the birth and after the birth of Christ.

While Our Blessed Mother is mentioned only a few times in the Gospels, her virginity is explicitly mentioned by both St. Luke and St. Matthew. In St. Luke's Gospel, Mary tells the angel that she is a virgin and has promised God to remain one. The angel confirms this. In St. Matthew's Gospel, Joseph confirms the fact that he is not the father of the Child in her womb. They are both told that the Child is conceived of the Holy Spirit.

> And Mary said to the angel, "How can this be, since I have no husband?" And the angel said to her, "The Holy Spirit will come upon you; therefore the child to be born will be called holy, the Son of God" (Lk 1:34−35).

> When his Mother Mary had been betrothed to Joseph, before they came together she was found to be with child of

the Holy Spirit; . . . an angel of the Lord appeared to him in a dream saying, ". . . that which is conceived in her is of the Holy Spirit . . ." (Mt 1:18—20).

Mary's virginity is given further testimony in the creeds. In the Apostles' Creed, we proclaim our belief in Jesus Christ, who "was conceived by the power of the Holy Spirit, born of the Virgin Mary. . . ." Similar statements are found in the Nicene Creed, as well as in many other prayers. This doctrine was formally defined at the Second Council of Constantinople in 553 A.D.

Assumption into Heaven

The third great privilege of Our Lady that we will discuss here is the doctrine of the *Assumption*. The Assumption means that Mary was taken, at the end of her earthly life, body and soul to Heaven. As in the case of her Immaculate Conception, she was unlike all other human beings in this respect. When we die, we know that our soul is separated from our body, and so we are not complete. We must wait until the end of the world for God to restore our bodies, in a glorified state, to us. This is one of the consequences that we bear because of original sin. Since Mary was conceived without original sin, it is fitting that God chose to spare the Mother of his Son this consequence of it.

Like the doctrine of the Immaculate Conception, this doctrine has been part of the Church's belief from the beginning. Since about the fifth century, the Eastern rites of the Church have celebrated the feast of the Assumption on August 15. However, it was not until 1950 that this doctrine was formally defined. On November 1 of that year, Pope Pius XII infallibly defined this doctrine. The feast of the Assumption, celebrated on August 15, is now a Holy Day of Obligation.

Mary in Our Lives

"Mary has by grace been exalted above all the angels and men to a place second only to her Son, as the most holy Mother of God who was involved in the mysteries of Christ; she is rightly honored by a special cult in the Church" (LG, 66).

In the Litany of Loreto (see the Appendix), we proclaim Mary as the Queen of angels and the Queen of saints. She has been exalted by God above all other creatures and now holds a place second to her Son, Christ, the King. Why should Mary be placed above even the angels? She has earned this honor because of her role in our salvation and her fullness of grace since the beginning of her life.

Because of Mary's place at the right hand of her Son, she should receive the proper veneration from us. We do not adore Our Lady, since adoration, or worship, is reserved for God alone. Rather, we *venerate* her above all other creatures because of her special place in our salvation. We believe that she is "full of grace" and as such is "blessed among women". Because of her place, it is fitting, as she herself proclaimed, that "all generations will call [her] blessed" (Lk 1:48).

In honoring Mary we also recognize that she is, as St. Pius X wrote, "our sure way to Christ". As our Mother, Mary *intercedes* in Heaven for us, as she did for others when she was on earth. Recall the story of Our Lord's first public miracle. Jesus and his disciples, together with Mary, were at a wedding in Cana. The host ran out of wine, and Mary turned to her Son, asking him to do something about it. And, as we know, Jesus granted her request; he would not refuse his Mother.

This episode teaches us an important lesson. Mary will continue to intercede with Jesus for her children. And Jesus, as he did at Cana, will listen to her pleas for us. Let us remember, then, to turn to Mary in prayer, asking her to give us through her Son the graces we need:

"O Mary, conceived without sin, pray for us, who have recourse to thee."

The Litany of Loreto: Our Lady's Litany

A litany is a form of prayer consisting of a series of petitions, each of which is followed by a fixed response. The litany begins by invoking the Persons of the Trinity and concludes with invocations of the Lamb of God. The body of the litany consists of petitions corresponding to a particular theme. The litanies that are formally recognized by the Church are the litanies to the Holy Name, the Sacred Heart, the Precious Blood, the Blessed Virgin, St. Joseph, and the saints.

The litany of the Blessed Virgin, known as the Litany of Loreto, is a series of invocations of the Blessed Virgin, each with the response, "Pray for us". It contains many beautiful titles of Our Lady and provides us with much to meditate. As you read and say this ancient prayer, which you will find in the Appendix, think about the meaning of each of Mary's titles.

"Yes, from this day forward all generations will call me blessed, for the Almighty has done great things for me."

(Lk 1:48)

Words to Know:

Annunciation   *Fiat*
Immaculate Conception
perpetual virginity   Assumption
venerate   intercede

Church Teaching

"This motherhood of Mary in the order of grace continues uninterruptedly from the consent which she loyally gave at the Annunciation and which she sustained without wavering beneath the Cross. . . . Taken up to Heaven she did not lay aside this saving office but by her manifold intercession continues to bring us the gifts of eternal salvation. By her maternal charity, she cares for the brethren of her Son, who still journey on earth surrounded by dangers and difficulties, until they are led into their blessed home" (LG, 62).

CHAPTER 10

The Communion of Saints

"Exactly as Christian communion between men on their earthly pilgrimage brings us closer to Christ, so our community with the saints joins us to Christ, from whom, as from its fountain and head, issues all grace and the life of the People of God itself" (LG, 50).

We have seen that the Church is the Mystical Body of Christ with Christ at its head and Mary as its Mother. We who have been baptized in Christ are the members. Membership in the Mystical Body is not limited to those living on earth. Since Baptism leaves us with a permanent character that can never be taken away, those who die faithful to their baptismal promises are still part of the Mystical Body. We use the term *Communion of Saints* to refer to the Church in this sense—as including her members both living and dead.

The term *saints* is used in various ways. In the widest sense, it means "holy ones"; all those who have been baptized share in the holiness of Christ. More specifically, saints means those who have died and are with God in Heaven. In the strictest sense the term refers to those who have been officially declared by the Church to be in Heaven—those we call the *canonized* saints. The union of these saints is based on our common possession of the life of grace and is expressed through the exchange of spiritual goods. Thus the Communion of

Saints includes all of the faithful who are united in Christ—the faithful on earth, the souls in Purgatory, and the *blessed*, or saints, in Heaven.

The Church Militant

The first part of the Communion of Saints is the faithful on earth. We are known as the *pilgrim Church* since we are journeying (on a pilgrimage) to Heaven. Sometimes we also refer to this group as the *Church Militant*. This indicates the "fight", or "struggle", that we on earth must constantly wage against sin and temptation.

Our unity is one of love. We are asked by Christ to carry one another's burdens, to serve each other, to help especially the least among us by the corporal and spiritual works of mercy. This is also done in a special way through prayers for each other. We frequently ask others to pray for us, or we join with them in praying for a particular need.

Intercessory prayer, prayer on behalf of another person, has long been a part of our religious heritage. In the *Old Testament* we often see the leaders and prophets of Israel pray to God for their people. When Our Lord was on earth we heard him pray to his Father for his disciples at the Last Supper. He also encouraged them to pray for one another and for those who would persecute them. In his

letters, St. Paul often asks the people to pray for him and mentions his own prayers for them. For example, in his letter to the Christian community in Rome he says ". . . without ceasing I mention you always in my prayers" (Rom 1:9). The Fathers and Doctors of the Church also frequently exhort us to pray for one another. In the Liturgy today the Church encourages us as well. In the *Prayer of the Faithful* at the end of the Liturgy of the Word, we pray expressly for the Church and the needs of its members.

The Church Suffering

Prayer for one another does not end with death. While those in Heaven do not need our prayers, those in Purgatory do, and we, the Church Militant, can and should pray for them as well. These souls in Purgatory represent the second part of the Communion of Saints and are known as the *Church Penitent* or *Church Suffering*.

When we die we do not all necessarily go straight to Heaven. Those who do go directly to Heaven love God perfectly and have no trace of sin left on their souls. Most of us, however, who die in the state of grace, still have some venial sins on our souls, or may not have sufficiently atoned for past sins, and some punishment due to sin may still be necessary.

The souls in this imperfect state not only need to be cleansed, but they want to be cleansed as well. They know that they are not yet prepared to be in the presence of God. Recalling one of Our Lord's parables may help us understand this:

> The Kingdom of Heaven may be compared to a king who gave a marriage feast for his son, . . . when the king came in to look at the guests, he saw there a man who had no wedding garment; and he

said to him, "Friend, how did you get in here without a wedding garment?" And he was speechless (Mt 22:2−12).

Just as the man who came to the wedding feast was required to have the proper garment, so we must be spotlessly clothed to enter the Kingdom of Heaven. If we are not we will, like the guest at the wedding, be "speechless" before our Heavenly King.

Those souls who need to be cleansed and purified before seeing God go to *Purgatory*. Purgatory is a place of temporary suffering that cleanses the soul and makes it worthy to see God. The Church's teaching on Purgatory is very consoling. Though we are sinful, God in his mercy gives us a chance to make up for these venial sins, and for the punishment still due for our confessed mortal sins. The principal suffering in Purgatory is not seeing God. Even though the souls in Purgatory really do suffer they are filled with peace because they are assured that they will be with God soon. They no longer fear for their salvation. They know that they are being made ready for Heaven.

The souls in Purgatory, however, are unable to do anything for themselves to shorten their time there. They depend on us, the Church Militant, to help them. We can do this by offering prayers for them, particularly the Mass, as well as offering other charitable acts. We can also offer our own sufferings here on earth for these souls.

Our Catholic practice of praying for those who have died is rooted in God's revelation to the Jews. In the *Old Testament*, the book of Maccabees tells the story of Judas Maccabeus, who lived in the second century before Christ. After a battle, it was discovered that some of his dead soldiers who were good men had sinned before their deaths. Judas Maccabeus then had prayers and sacrifices offered to God for these men: ". . . It was a holy and pious thought . . . he made atonement for the dead, that they might be delivered from their sin'' (2 Macc 12:45).

In this passage God reveals to us that our prayers can help those who have died. It was also the belief of the early Christians and is part of Tradition. In many ancient Christian tombs we find inscriptions which encourage prayers for those who are buried there.

Because prayer for those who have died is so important, the Church sets aside one day each year on which the whole Church prays for the souls in Purgatory. This is All Souls' Day and is celebrated on November 2. The month of November is dedicated to prayers for those who have died, particularly our own family members and friends.

We should not forget the souls in Purgatory during the remainder of the year, particularly at Mass, during the Eucharistic prayer when we pray for the dead. But we should try to do this at other times as well. For example, many Catholics add the following short prayer to their prayer before or after meals:

"May the souls of the faithful departed, through the mercy of God, rest in peace. *Amen.*"

There are other things as well that can help us remember to pray for those who have died. Often holy cards are distributed at funerals. The purpose of these cards is to remind us to pray for the person who has died. As pictures in our homes remind us to think of our family members who have died, so, too, these holy cards remind us of them. We should keep them some place where they can remind us to pray for the faithful departed.

The Church Triumphant

The blessed in Heaven can also pray for the souls in Purgatory, as well as for us on earth. They are the third part of the Communion of Saints—the *Church Triumphant*. They are triumphant because they have completely conquered sin and now share in eternal glory, even before the resurrection of their bodies.

Among the blessed in Heaven are the *canonized* saints, whom the Church has officially declared to be in Heaven. As we have seen, the most important among these is Our Lady, But there are also many others who have reached Heaven—perhaps some of our own relatives and friends—and deserve to be called saints as well. We do not know for certain who they are, but the Church honors them with a feast each year—the feast of All Saints on November 1.

All these are saints in glory with Christ, who, shining like stars in the firmament, are ''in front of the throne and in front of the Lamb'' (Rev 7:9). We are ultimately united with them in our love and union in Christ, and in the grace he gives us. In our prayers, especially in the Liturgy of the Church, we join their heavenly chorus in the glorification of God, saying:

Blessing and glory and wisdom and thanksgiving and honor and power and might be to our God for ever and ever. *Amen* (Rev 7:12).

We are not just praying alone, each member of the Church by himself. We are united in a community of incomparable grandeur, in a victorious union of love. This great community lifts us up and generates fruits of grace in us.

We partake in this Communion of Saints, and we can turn to the saints for help, just as we turn to other members of the Church on earth. We ask them to intercede with God for us, just as we might ask a friend here to do the same.

We should remember that we are not worshipping the saints, but praying to God *through them.*

The saints are truly united with us through Christ and want to help us. St. Thérèse of Lisieux remarked before her death that she would "spend her Heaven doing good upon earth". And this is what the saints do when we turn to them.

We are also honoring God when we venerate the saints. The saints are masterpieces of God's grace. Grace has triumphed in them and the devil has been conquered. In venerating them we honor God, whose life shines forth in them.

Devotion to the saints goes back to the early days of the Church. The early Christians began to honor the apostles after their deaths, and later the martyrs were included as well. Gradually, the practice was extended to other holy men and women. The Church recognized their holiness and saw that they could be examples to the faithful. The saints show us that we can reach Heaven, and they show us the way.

The saints came from all walks of life—some were married with families, some were priests or Religious Sisters or Brothers, some were kings or queens, some were rich and others poor. Yet, they all had their complete devotion to God in common. Since their lives were so different, it is not surprising that we might find the life of one saint more interesting or helpful to us than another. People, in fact, often develop a devotion to particular saints.

For example, the people of one country may have a devotion to a particular saint whose life was intimately connected with their nation. St. Patrick spread the Catholic faith throughout Ireland, and because of this he is the *patron saint* of Ireland. St. Thomas More was a great lawyer and statesman in England. He is the patron saint of all lawyers and also the patron saint of all laypeople because he served God as a layman. We might also have a special devotion to the saint for whom we were named.

Because the lives of the saints are such important examples for us, in the next two chapters we will briefly examine a few of them. This will also give us a chance to see something of the history of the Church as we look at the times in which they lived.

Words to Know:

Communion of Saints
Church Triumphant
Church Suffering   pilgrim Church
Church Militant   intercessory prayer
patron saint   canonized saint

Q. 19   *What is Purgatory?*

Purgatory is the temporary suffering of the lack of the vision of God and of other punishments, which remove from the soul the remains of sin, making it worthy of seeing God.

Q. 20   *Can we help and even liberate souls from the pains of Purgatory?*

We can help and even liberate souls from the pains of Purgatory with good works—our prayers, indulgences, alms, and other good works, especially by means of the Holy Mass.

Q. 21 *What does "Communion of Saints" mean?*

The Communion of Saints means that all the faithful, who form one single body in Jesus Christ, share in all the good that exists and is done in this same body, namely, in the universal Church.

Q. 22 *Do the blessed and the souls in Purgatory form a part of the Communion of Saints?*

The blessed in Heaven and the souls in Purgatory do form a part of the Communion of Saints, because they are joined to each other and with us by charity, because those in Paradise receive our prayers and those in Purgatory our assistance, and because they all repay us with their intercession with God on our behalf.

Q. 23 *If God hears him who prays well, why do we invoke also Our Lady, the angels, and the saints?*

We invoke Our Lady, the angels, and the saints because they are dear to God, Our Lord, and full of kindness toward us. Hence they help us in our requests by their powerful intercession.

Q. 24 *Why are the angels, the saints, and Our Lady powerful intercessors with God?*

The angels and the saints are powerful intercessors with God because they are his faithful servants and moreover his much-beloved friends. Our Lady is the most powerful intercessor of all, because she is the Mother of God and full of grace. This is why we invoke her so frequently, and all the more because Jesus Christ left her to us as our Mother.

Q. 25 *Does not the invocation of Our Lady and the saints perhaps manifest lack of confidence in Jesus Christ, the only Mediator, as if his merits did not suffice to obtain for us the graces we need?*

Invoking Our Lady and the saints does not in any sense manifest a lack of confidence in Jesus Christ, the only Mediator. On the contrary, prayer to these intercessors manifests a greater faith in his merits, which are so great and so efficacious that through them, and only through them, Our Lady and the other saints obtain from God their grace, their own merits, and their power of intercession.

CHAPTER 11

Saints in Our History: The First Thousand Years

"And his gifts were that some should be apostles, some prophets, some evangelists, some pastors and teachers, for the equipment of the saints, for the work of ministry, for building up the body of Christ, until we all attain to the unity of faith and of the knowledge of the Son of God" (Eph 4:11 − 13).

Almost two thousand years have elapsed since the founding of the Church and its birth on Pentecost. As we have seen, it began as a small community, but like the mustard seed in the parable, it has grown and spread throughout the world. During that time it has faced many difficulties and weathered many storms. Yet the Church has survived and is today the same Church of which Our Lord spoke when he said to Peter, ". . . on this rock I will build my Church, and the powers of death shall not prevail against it" (Mt 16:18).

The Church could not have survived without the constant guidance and protection of the Holy Spirit. In order to preserve the Church God has raised up many holy men and women who are today recognized as *saints*. With God's help they have been able to put their various talents and personalities in the service of the Church's special need.

The virtuous lives of these saints are still a source of example and inspiration for us today. Let us now look at a few periods in the Church's history as they are reflected in the lives of some of her greatest saints.

Apostles and Martyrs

The early days of the Church were marked by the apostles carrying out Our Lord's command: "Go therefore and make disciples of all nations" (Mt 28:19). This *missionary* activity manifests the Church's universality. We have seen that right after Pentecost Peter went out to preach, and by the end of the day three thousand persons were baptized. He was imprisoned, suffered, labored, performed miracles in the name of Jesus, and continued to preach and speak with authority.

Later he went to Antioch and finally to Rome, where he stayed permanently. Peter thus became the first bishop of Rome. He was martyred under the Roman Emperor Nero around the year 64 or 67 A.D. It is said that when they were crucifying him Peter said he was not worthy to die as his Master had died, and therefore he asked that the crucifix be turned upside down. He was buried on the command to teach *all* nations, he is called the "Apostle to the Gentiles". Like many of the early Christians, St. Paul not only lived for Christ; around 68 A.D. he died for him as well, as a martyr.

Although the Church continued her missionary work, the next 250 years were characterized by the persecution of Christians. As their numbers increased, and Christianity spread throughout the Roman Empire, the Roman government began to fear the Church. Under certain emperors over the next two centuries, many Christians were put to death for their faith in Christ. Those who died giving witness to their faith were called *martyrs*, the Greek word for witness. Many of them were young and only recently baptized, while still others had only heard and accepted the message but had not yet been baptized. Yet they all had one thing in common: they willingly accepted horrible tortures and death rather than deny Christ or his message.

These martyrs were an inspiration both to their fellow Christians and to many Roman citizens. In fact, many people were drawn to the faith after seeing those who willingly died for it. They realized that the Christian faith must be great if so many Christians were willing to give up their lives for its sake. The rapid growth of the Church during this period led one early Christian writer to remark that the "blood of the martyrs is the seed of the Church".

Among those whose blood nourished the Church were two young women who lived in the early third century, St. Perpetua and St. Felicity. Perpetua, a young married woman, was from a wealthy family in Carthage, North Africa. Felicity was a young servant in her household. Shortly after Perpetua gave birth to a baby, she and other members of her household, including Felicity, were arrested because they were Christians. Despite her family's pleas that she give up her faith and return home to her

Vatican Hill. St. Peter's Basilica was later built over his tomb. Pope St. Linus was elected to succeed him.

The greatest missionary of these early days is the apostle St. Paul. From the time of his conversion, which is described in the Acts of the Apostles, St. Paul preached throughout Palestine, Syria, parts of Asia Minor (modern-day Turkey), Greece, and Rome. During four missionary journeys he zealously preached the good news of Jesus Christ to the Jews and, most importantly, to the *gentiles* (non-Jews). In some places he endured bitter opposition— for example, he was stoned and imprisoned— but still he continued to preach.

In the fourteen letters that he wrote to the communities where he preached, as well as in the accounts of his journeys found in the Acts, we can see St. Paul's great devotion to Christ. Because he so fully carried out Our Lord's child, Perpetua refused and remained strong.

Felicity, who was awaiting the birth of her own child, was eager to join Perpetua in facing death for Christ. The Roman law, however, would not allow a woman who was with child to be put to death. Because Felicity's child was born soon after her imprisonment, she was martyred along with her mistress and the others who had been arrested with them. The willingness of both Perpetua and Felicity to die for Christ—even though they were young women with children they loved—shows us that they placed God first in their lives.

We honor the memories of St. Perpetua and St. Felicity when we ask their intercession during the Eucharistic prayer of the Mass. We also invoke the intercession of many of the other martyrs here. Among them are the first martyr, Stephen; several early Popes: Linus, Cletus, Clement, and Sixtus; several holy women: Agatha, Lucy, and Cecilia; and the apostles.

In the same way that the early Christians were inspired by the faith of the martyrs, we too look to them as examples of courage. We also can look to the martyrs of our own times. For although the early centuries of the Church were the age of martyrs, we still have many people who have died—and are dying—for their faith.

Fathers and Doctors of the Church

The great age of martyrdom ended in the early fourth century, when the Roman emperor Constantine issued a decree allowing Christians to practice their religion freely. Once this occurred, Christians were able to preach the gospel in the open. Even though the Church was freed from one problem, she soon had to face others. Trouble now came from within the Church in the form of *heresies*. A heresy is a denial of a basic doctrine of the faith. Those who hold and teach heresies are called *heretics*.

At the time when Constantine became emperor, a major heresy was being preached in Egypt by a priest named Arius. Arius taught that Jesus Christ, the Son of God, was not of the same nature as the Father. In other words, he said that Jesus was not God.

Because Arius was a forceful speaker and persuasive writer, his heresy, called the Arian heresy, spread rapidly through the Church and even deceived many bishops and priests. Because this heresy denied one of the most fundamental doctrines of our faith, it had to be stopped. The first step was the Church council that met in Nicaea in 325 A.D.

One of the bishops who fought to defend the truth during and after that council was *St. Athanasius*. Athanasius was the bishop of Alexandria in Egypt, where he defended the teaching of the Church against many Arian forces. He faced several threats to his life and was exiled for his defense of orthodoxy. Despite all of this, he never wavered in defending the truth that the Son of God is "one in being with the Father".

Many of Athanasius' writings concern the doctrine he defended throughout his life. One of his books, *On the Incarnation*, is a treatise on the mystery of the Second Person of the Trinity made flesh. When he died in 373 A.D., Arianism had not been completely conquered. His efforts, however, were not in vain, and Arianism was finally defeated by 381 A.D.

Other heresies, many of which also concerned the nature of Christ, followed the Arian heresy. Saints were raised up to defend the Church against these heresies as well. One of the greatest saints to defend the Church was *St. Augustine*, who was born near the end of Athanasius' life. Although Augustine became one of the greatest bishops, teachers, and *theologians* (persons who study and teach about God) in the Church, his early life reminds us that even great sinners who repent can become saints.

Born in North Africa, Augustine was the son of a Roman official and a Christian woman named Monica. During his youth he showed that he had a brilliant mind and was recognized as a great student. In his adolescence, however, he acquired many bad habits and lived a wild life; he seriously broke the Commandment on purity. His mother patiently prayed for him, begging God to give him the grace to accept the faith and reform his life.

Her prayers were answered when, after many years of searching for the truth, Augustine was baptized at the age of thirty-three. Later he became a priest and eventually a bishop. During the remainder of his life he preached many sermons and wrote over one hundred books in defense of the faith. Among these books is his own story of his life and his conversion, *The Confessions*. Another book, which many consider his most famous work, is *The City of God*, which contrasts the life of the Christian with the evils of the world in which we must live. Like St. Athanasius, St. Augustine, who died in 430 A.D., is considered one of the Fathers of the Church.

The Monasteries

Later, in the fifth century, *barbarian* tribes began to threaten the stability of the Roman Empire. The barbarians were warlike, uncivilized tribes living in northern Europe outside the boundaries of the empire. As they expanded, they moved south and began invading the empire, once even threatening the city of Rome. The Church recognized the need to convert them to Christianity and to civilize them.

Much of this work was performed during the next three centuries by the monks and the *monasteries*. Monks were men who lived a life of poverty, chastity, and obedience together

in order to serve Christ. They lived according to a specific *rule*, or way of life, in communities that were usually in remote areas. Here they supported themselves through agricultural activity and dedicated their time to God. Gradually they formed schools at their monasteries. It was through these schools and their later missionary work that the monks were able to Christianize and educate much of Europe.

Although there were monks in the Church as early as the third century, the title of "Father of Western Monasticism" is given to St. Benedict, who was born in 480 A.D. He established the famous monastery at Monte Cassino in Italy and is the founder of the Benedictine order. He composed a rule, which we call the *rule of St. Benedict* to guide the daily activities of his monks.

Benedict divided the daily activities of his monks into prayer and physical work. This became the motto of all Benedictines: *Ora et Labora* (pray and work). The daily prayer consisted of the Divine Office—chanted together at seven specific hours of the day and night—and the daily Sacrifice of the Mass. The labor, which was also considered a form of prayer, was both manual—farming, building, and so on—and intellectual—copying of manuscripts, writing books, educating, and the like.

As time passed, the monasteries were not only centers of learning but also missionary centers, from which monks set out to spread the faith. Among these missionary monks was St. Columban, an Irishman who preached the faith among the Franks (living in the area of modern-day France) during the end of the sixth century. Another great example was St. Boniface, a Benedictine monk from England. In the eighth century he left England for the area of Germany. For many years Boniface preached there, spreading the faith and baptizing many from the Germanic tribes.

The Church Faces Problems

While the monks were busy Christianizing the barbarians in Europe, the Church was faced with other invasions as well. A new religion, Islam, had emerged in Arabia early in the seventh century and was now being spread throughout North Africa and the eastern portion of the old Roman Empire. The followers of Islam, called Moslems, eventually gained control of the Mediterranean Sea. As a result, Christians living in western Europe were physically separated from those in the East.

This event intensified problems that had existed for a long time. Christians in the two parts of the empire were divided by language and culture. There had also been a long-running debate over the wording of certain doctrines and over the authority of the bishop of Rome (the Pope). These problems were finally brought to a head in 1054 A.D. In that year, the Church in the East formally separated itself from the Pope and the Roman Catholic Church. This is known as the Eastern *schism*, or split. While *some* of the Eastern Christians have been reunited with the Church—for example, the Byzantine Catholics—the schism still exists today.

This schism was only one great problem that the Church faced as it completed its first thousand years. A second was the great corruption of the clergy during the *Dark Ages*. This period, from about 850–1000 A.D., was the result of the gradual collapse of the old Roman Empire. As the Empire collapsed, the Church was the only stable force remaining in the world. Because few laymen were educated, it was left to the clergy to take up the responsibility of governing civil society. Many Church leaders then exercised not only spiritual but temporal power as well.

After a while many bishops, priests, and monks began to forget their roles as spiritual leaders. Unfortunately they became far too concerned with their temporal affairs or their own possessions and lost sight of their primary task. Sad to say, there were even Popes who, though they never taught error, were sinful, corrupt, and worldly. The need for reform of the clergy became more and more urgent. Once again, many saints rose up during the next few centuries to guide the Church through its next crisis.

Words to Know:

St. Athanasius
St. Augustine   St. Benedict
gentiles   martyrs   heresy
barbarian   monasteries
theologian

CHAPTER 12

Saints in Our History: The Second Thousand Years

"Exactly as Christian communion between men on their earthly pilgrimage brings us closer to Christ, so our community with the saints joins us to Christ, from whom as from its fountain and head issues all grace and the life of the People of God itself" (LG, 50).

As the Church moved into the eleventh and twelfth centuries, one of its first concerns was reforming the corrupt clergy. Fortunately, the Church was blessed with several holy Popes, who were able to begin these reforms.

Other holy men began to reform the monasteries. The most important of these is St. Bernard of Clairvaux. As a young man Bernard joined a new monastic community known as the Cistercians, whose way of life was based on the rule of St. Benedict. But their way of life was simpler and stricter than that in most Benedictine communities of the time.

After he was ordained, Bernard was chosen to begin a new monastery following the Cistercian way of life. Bernard became the abbot of this monastery at Clairvaux and then founded sixty-eight more monasteries according to the same rule. The new generation of monasteries corrected many of the abuses that had crept into monastic life during the Dark Ages, and these monasteries were a great source of hope.

St. Bernard's own holiness was reflected in the life of Clairvaux and the other monasteries. He strengthened the faith by his sermons about devotion to Jesus and to his Mother. So great were these sermons that people from all over Europe came to hear him. Thus St. Bernard was able to rekindle the faith of the laity as well as that of his monks.

The Crusades

He had great influence on other matters in Europe as well. For example, St. Bernard preached the second Crusade, encouraging many people in France and Germany to join. The *Crusades* were the response of the Church to a new difficulty that had arisen because of the Moslems.

Toward the end of the eleventh century, the Moslems seized control of the *Holy Land* (Palestine) and persecuted those Christians who traveled on pilgrimages to Jerusalem and the other holy places. The Crusades were military efforts to win back the Holy Land. They were carried on periodically during the next two centuries. The knights and soldiers who fought those battles for the cause of Christ used the Cross as their symbol. Many who either led or fought these Crusades were truly saintly men.

One of these courageous men was King St. Louis IX of France, who led the last two major Crusades. He is noted for being a holy man and a just ruler. His devotion to his faith was instilled in him at an early age by his mother. When he was growing up she often said to him, "I love you, my dear son, as much as a mother can love her child, but I would rather see you dead at my feet than that you should commit a mortal sin." Such lessons never left him, even when he became the king of France.

While he was king, he attended two Masses each day and spent much of his time in prayer. He frequently cared for the poor personally, often having them join his family at meals. And he taught his sons to love their faith as well. In his last words to his eldest son he wrote, ". . . the first thing I would teach thee is to set thine heart to love God".

For St. Louis, as for any saint, love of God came first. Thus, when it seemed necessary to fight a battle for Christ, St. Louis readily responded. He died on his way to fight his second Crusade. His last words echoed those of Our Lord on the Cross, "Into thy hands I commend my spirit."

Despite their great efforts, the Crusaders did not finally achieve their goal. The Holy Land was not freed from the Moslems. The Crusades did, however, strengthen the faith of many in Europe and increase devotion to Christ and his saints. They also opened western Europe to many areas of knowledge in which the Moslems had advanced—for example, navigation, medicine, and philosophy. This provided the basis for many scholarly and scientific achievements during the next few centuries.

The internal reforms of the Church, begun by St. Bernard and others, grew and flourished during the thirteenth century. This was the height of the period known as the *Middle Ages*.

New Religious Orders

During this century, two new religious orders were founded that were dramatically different from the traditional orders. The members of these communities did not live in monasteries isolated from society but lived instead in the towns where they worked. Unlike the monastic communities, which owned large portions of land to support themselves, these new orders depended on the generosity of ordinary people for their basic needs. They are called *mendicant* orders, because they lived by begging. By living simply, these orders reminded Christians that the true role of the religious was to serve God.

The first of these communities was the Franciscan order, which was founded in Italy by *St. Francis of Assisi*. Francis, the son of a wealthy merchant in Assisi, grew up with plenty of money, which he spent recklessly. He wanted to become a knight but realized that Christ was calling him to serve God in the religious life. Francis then decided to live as a poor man, discarding his fine clothes for those of a beggar and caring for the needy and the sick.

He began a life of prayer—preaching and serving the poor. His holiness attracted many young men, who joined him in his work. Eventually Francis wrote a simple rule for his followers. With the Pope's blessing they were established as the Order of Friars Minor ("Little Brothers"). By the time of Francis' death, there were over five thousand Franciscans in Europe.

Men were not the only ones attracted to Francis' way of life. A rich young woman from Assisi also asked to join him, and thus with Francis' help St. Clare established a community for women, who also lived according to the Franciscan rule.

Another mendicant order for men was founded by a young Spanish priest, Dominic de Guzman.

This order is known as the Dominicans, or Order of Preachers. As a young priest *St. Dominic* was sent to convert a group of heretics living in southern France, the Albigensians. To help him in this task, he gathered a group of young men who were willing to dedicate themselves to preaching. Like the Franciscans, they lived in simplicity and poverty. They spent their time in teaching and preaching. The Dominicans emphasized scholarly learning for their members, so that they would be able to preach more effectively. Consequently, many of the great university teachers of this age were Dominicans.

St. Thomas Aquinas

The greatest of these Dominican scholars and teachers was *St. Thomas Aquinas*. Thomas was born in Italy in 1225 A.D. and began his education at the Benedictine monastery at Monte Cassino. His wealthy family hoped that one day he would become a Benedictine. Thomas went on to study at the University of Naples, where he first met the Dominicans. Their simple life of poverty and study attracted Thomas, and, despite many vigorous objections from his family, he joined the order.

He studied theology and philosophy with another Dominican, St. Albert the Great, and eventually became a teacher himself at the University of Paris.

Thomas studied the ancient Greek philosopher Aristotle, whose writings were among those brought back to Europe by the Crusaders. St. Thomas used Aristotle's ideas in his own work in theology. He taught that God's revelation to man is not contrary to reason but, rather, that reason is necessary to understand God more completely. While his method was based on Aristotle, his insights were based on the Scriptures and the writings of the Fathers. He wrote a large number of books, but the best known and most important of these is his *Summa Theologiae*. In this famous book he organized, explained, and defended all the doctrines of our faith. Thomas' writings have never been surpassed in the Church and remain today among the most important sources for Catholic theology.

Although Thomas' scholarly works were important to the Church, it was his love of God that made him a saint. His devotion to Christ and the Blessed Sacrament are reflected in some of the beautiful prayers and poems he composed for certain feasts. For example, St. Thomas wrote the beautiful hymn *Pange Lingua* ("Sing My Tongue"), the final verses of which are frequently sung at Benediction. Christ and the Church were the center of St. Thomas' life, and he knew that his writings were unimportant compared to the infinite wisdom of God.

In 1274 A.D. St. Thomas was asked by the Pope to attend the Church council in Lyons,

France. While on his way he became ill and died on March 7, 1274. Before he died, he displayed his humility and love for God. As he prepared to receive the Eucharist for the last time, he said:

> I receive thee, price of my redemption, Viaticum of my pilgrimage, for love of whom I have fasted, prayed, taught, and labored. Never have I said a word against thee. If I have it was in ignorance and I do not persist in my ignorance. I leave the correction of my work to the Holy Catholic Church, and in that obedience I pass from this life.

St. Catherine of Siena

Although the Church flourished in the thirteenth century, it suffered many problems in the centuries that followed. During the fourteenth century debates between the Popes and the kings of France created a major crisis. For the first time since St. Peter, the Pope was not in Rome. For seventy years the Popes lived in the French city of Avignon. It was a woman from Siena, Italy, who finally persuaded the Pope that he must return to Rome.

St. Catherine of Siena was a young laywoman who had chosen to live a life of prayer and service to others, particularly the sick. Her reputation for holiness spread throughout Italy, and many people turned to her for help and advice.

Several times Catherine wrote to Pope Gregory XI, urging him to return to Rome for the good of the Church. Finally, she visited him in Avignon, pointing out to him that many of the Church's problems stemmed from the absence of the Popes from Rome. Pope Gregory listened to her, returned to Rome, and began to reform the Church. Catherine died only a few years later at the age of thirty-three. Because of her many spiritual writings, Catherine was declared a Doctor of the Church.

Although St. Catherine helped the Church end one crisis, another, even greater, followed almost immediately. For the next forty years there were two men, one in Avignon and one in Rome, who claimed to be Pope. This confusion, known as the *Great Western Schism*, divided the Church and weakened the role of the Pope. By the time it was resolved, the Church's unity was threatened.

Protestant Reformation

The fifteenth century also brought with it many new developments. This age is known as the *Renaissance* (rebirth) because of the renewed interest in the ancient Greek and Roman civilizations. During this time many of the clergy were once again corrupted by money and other luxuries. Also, the invention of the printing press made it possible for new ideas—

some heretical—to spread more rapidly. By the beginning of the sixteenth century, the Church was once more in need of reform.

Unfortunately, some attempts to reform the Church led the "reformers" away from her. This is known as the *Protestant Reformation*. Beginning with Martin Luther, several groups rebelled and broke away from the Church. This was the beginning of the many Christian denominations we see around us today.

This tremendous upheaval was the reason that the Church called the Council of Trent. The Church did need reform, and she also needed to clarify the doctrines that were being challenged by the Protestants. The work of this council strengthened the Church so that she emerged from her latest crisis stronger and more able to face the work ahead.

The period immediately following the council is known as the *Counter-Reformation*. Just as new religious orders had helped the Church to reform during the Middle Ages, likewise new religious orders helped the Church to renew herself at this time. For example, the Ursuline sisters, dedicated to teaching young women, were formed by St. Angela Merici. The most important of these new communities was the Society of Jesus (the Jesuits), founded by *St. Ignatius of Loyola*.

St. Ignatius of Loyola

St. Ignatius was a Spanish nobleman who was trained to be a soldier. During his career, he became noted for his bravery and loyalty to his king. In one battle he was seriously wounded and required several months' rest. During this time he read the only books that were available to him—a life of Christ and some lives of the saints. By the time his leg had healed, his life had changed. St. Ignatius vowed to become a "soldier" in the service of Christ and his Church.

After a time of spiritual retreat, Ignatius began to study theology to prepare himself for his new work. While he was studying at the University of Paris, he was joined by other young men, and together they made their first vows of poverty and chastity. After a few years they formed themselves into an order and offered their services to the Pope.

The special work of the Society of Jesus was to defend the faith and serve the Church in whatever way or place the Pope asked them. At the beginning this took the form of defending the faith against the attacks of the Protestants. For example, many Jesuits were sent to Germany to preach against Lutheranism, and they were successful in bringing many people back to the Church. As time passed, the Society began to establish its own universities, convinced that a strong Catholic education would ensure loyalty to the Church.

The motto of St. Ignatius and his Society was "*Ad Majorem Dei Gloriam*" ("to the greater glory of God"). He really lived only for God's glory, and that eventually made him a saint.

Missionaries to the New World

In the centuries that followed, the Church, strong and healthy once more, began to spread even further. The European nations had begun to explore and colonize territories in Asia, Africa, and the Americas. The Church also was active, spreading the faith to the people in these areas. The greatest missionary activity since the early days of the Church followed the Reformation.

One of the greatest missionaries at this time was a Jesuit, St. Francis Xavier. He was among the original members of the Society of Jesus and was chosen by St. Ignatius to be one of the Society's first missionaries. Like the great missionary St. Paul, Francis covered a vast territory in a very short time.

His preaching began in India. From there he traveled through Sri Lanka, Malaysia (Indonesia), and Japan, converting many as he went. He died before he could enter China, but future Jesuits who continued his work did preach the gospel in China. The work begun by St. Francis Xavier paved the way for later missionaries to the Orient.

Jesuit missionaries from France were among those who brought the message of Christ to the French territories in North America. St. Isaac Jogues and seven others are called the "North American martyrs". They preached among the Indians and suffered martyrdom for their faith.

Spanish missionaries labored in the southwestern and western portions of the North American continent. One of the most notable is the Franciscan priest Fr. Junipero Serra, who founded a series of missions among the Indians in California.

With the work of the missionaries and Catholics who settled in America from Europe, the faith was planted on American soil. The first saint born in the United States was St. Elizabeth Seton, who was born in 1774.

Elizabeth was raised as an Episcopalian and married William Seton, a prosperous merchant from New York. They had five children. When Elizabeth's husband became ill with tuberculosis, they moved to Italy, where he died. In Italy Elizabeth became convinced that the Roman Catholic Church was the true Church.

When she returned home, Elizabeth became a Catholic, despite the strong objections of her family and friends. To support herself and her children she opened a school for other young children in her vicinity and later in Maryland. Her school was unusual because it was intended for any student, not just the children of the rich. This was the beginning of the Catholic school system in the United States.

Other young women joined her. In time this group became a religious community, the Sisters of Charity. Founded in 1809, this was the first religious order to be founded in America.

During this time of missionary expansion, the Church was challenged by the scientific, intellectual, and political revolutions taking place in Europe. The Church was constantly called upon to defend herself but was able to remain strong.

Modern Times

As the Church entered the twentieth century, she was blessed with a saintly Pope, Pius X. A simple country priest, but also a great teacher, Pius was able to help the Church face one of the greatest heresies in her history—*Modernism*. Modernists think that teachings on faith and morals should change and evolve, and that there is no unchangeable, objective revelation from God on which Christianity is based. In addition, modernists deny the reality of supernatural events, such as miracles, which support the Christian faith. Pope Pius X wrote two great encyclicals summarizing and refuting these ideas.

Pope St. Pius served as a great shepherd of the Church. He encouraged frequent reception of Holy Communion. He reminded Catholics that the Eucharist is our spiritual food. He also lowered the age at which young children may first receive this great sacrament. In addition, Pope Pius X encouraged the Catholic laity to become involved in charitable work among the poor. He died broken hearted as the First World War began, expressing his simplicity in his last will and testament, "I was born poor, I lived poor, I die poor."

Since his death, the Church and the world have faced more challenges—particularly the spread of *atheistic*, *totalitarian* forms of government in various nations. The two world wars since the death of Pius X remind us of the terrible evils of *Nazism*, *communism*, and *fascism*. In opposition to these evils, one of the great saints of this century, St. Maximilian Kolbe, shines forth as an example for our times.

Maximilian was born in Poland near the turn of the century. As a member of the Franciscan order, he devoted much of his time and intelligence to understanding the role of Our Lady in our salvation. Before he was ordained, he organized a group of the friars into what he called the "Knights of Mary Immaculate". Members of this group dedicated themselves to win the whole world for Mary. After his ordination, he also gathered lay people into his group. In order to spread his message further, in the early 1920s he began a magazine called *The Knight of the Immaculate*. He had no financial backing, but the magazine thrived surprisingly, although it continually faced financial difficulties. He also established a community in Nagasaki, Japan, which later miraculously survived the atom bomb.

In 1936, after establishing the community in Japan, Maximilian returned to Poland. At this time Hitler came to power in Germany, and soon his armies invaded Poland. Maximilian was arrested by the Gestapo and imprisoned in Auschwitz in 1941.

Maximilian was immediately a source of strength for all imprisoned with him. Shortly after he arrived, some prisoners escaped from the camp. In retaliation, the Nazis randomly chose ten prisoners to be starved to death. One man who was chosen, Sgt. Francis Gajowniczek, began to cry for his wife and children. At this point Fr. Maximilian asked the guards if he could take the sergeant's place. When asked why he chose to do this, he answered, "I am a Catholic priest." With that Maximilian Kolbe began the road to his martyrdom. He prayed and gave courage to the other nine men in the starvation bunker. To the complete surprise of the Nazi guards, he was still alive after three weeks of neither food nor water, and they finally killed him. St. Maximilian died as he had lived—offering his life to God.

In our times the Church continues to grow, as the faith is spread in places such as India and Africa. After two thousand years we see that the Holy Spirit continues to guide the Church. Christ's promise continues: ". . . the powers of death shall not prevail against it."

Words to Know:

St. Francis of Assisi
St. Catherine of Siena
St. Dominic   St. Thomas Aquinas
Crusades   Middle Ages
Great Western Schism   Renaissance
Reformation   Counter-Reformation
St. Ignatius of Loyola   Modernism

CHAPTER 13

Separated Brethren

"I, therefore, a prisoner for the Lord, beg you to lead a life worthy of the calling to which you have been called, with all lowliness and meekness, with patience, forbearing one another in love, eager to maintain the unity of the Spirit in the bond of peace" (Eph 4:1 −3).

The universality of the Church is manifested in our times by the millions of Catholics throughout the world. At the same time, there are still many people who do not belong to the Catholic Church yet are members of various organized religions. Of these people, some believe in Christ, while others do not, even though they believe in the one, true God. There are others who may have some sort of religion but do not believe in the one, true God. All of these people are outside the visible Church, but in varying degrees. In this chapter we will consider their relationship to the Church.

> Let us pray for all our brothers and sisters who share our faith in Jesus Christ, that God may gather and keep together in one Church all those who seek the truth with sincerity (*General Intercession from the Liturgy of Good Friday*).

Those closest to the Church are non-Catholic Christians who have been baptized. They are often referred to as our *separated brethren*. They are united in some way to the Mystical Body in virtue of their Baptism. This is because there is but "one Baptism for the forgiveness of sins", as we profess in the Nicene Creed. We are all baptized in Christ. Thus anyone who has received the sacrament of Baptism has been united to Christ and his Body, the Church.

What divides Christians, however, is the degree to which they accept the teachings and practices handed down through the apostles from Christ. It is only the Catholic Church that teaches the full message of Our Lord. The divisions in belief and practice among Christians vary by degrees.

Those who are closest to the Church are the Orthodox Christians, who possess all of the sacraments but who have separated themselves from the authority of the Church. They did this, as we saw, one thousand years ago when they rejected the authority of the Pope.

In the next place are those denominations that broke away from the Church at the time of the Reformation—for example, the Lutherans. In addition to separating themselves from the authority of the Church, these groups also rejected certain teachings and sacraments of the Church. The Lutherans, for example, rejected the need for the sacrament of Penance and taught that individuals may interpret the Scriptures without the guidance of the Church.

Finally, there are Christian denominations that have broken from these groups, rejecting still more doctrines of our faith. Since the Reformation, new Christian denominations

have continued to appear, as people decided to keep certain parts of the message of Christ while rejecting others.

While all of these various Christian groups possess some parts of Christ's gospel, they are still separated from the fullness of his message.

The fullness of unity in the Church requires that all Christians be united again in doctrine and worship. The Church prays for this, especially in the Liturgy of Good Friday. The message of the prayer is that those united to Christ, initially in Baptism, may be fully united with him in faith.

Almighty and eternal God, long ago you gave your promise to Abraham and his posterity. Listen to your Church as we pray that the people you first made your own may arrive at the fullness of redemption (*General Intercession from the Liturgy of Good Friday*).

Then there are those people who do not believe in Christ, but who do believe in the one, true God. These are the Jews and the Moslems. The Jews, by virtue of their history, bear a closer relationship with the Church.

The Jews were the first *chosen people*. God first revealed himself to man when he made the Covenant with Abraham. He promised that Abraham's descendants would be his special people and that he would be their God.

Over the centuries God gradually revealed himself to these people, preparing them specially for his spiritual Kingdom, which was still to come. God revealed to his people that salvation would come to the world through them. God promised that he would restore to the world the harmony and closeness to God that had existed before the Fall. This would be accomplished by a descendant of Abraham—the Messiah.

When they had been instructed and formed,

the Jews were ready to receive the fullness of God's revelation. They were ready to be transformed into the wholly spiritual people God had intended them to be. And so Jesus Christ, the Son of God, came into the world.

Many of the Jews, however, did not recognize him as the Messiah. Because of this, they are separated from the Church today. They should be members of the Church, for salvation came from them. Jesus himself said to the Samaritan woman at the well, ''Salvation comes from the Jews'' (Jn 4:22). A special bond unites us with them. Jesus sprang from their own stock; he was ''Son of David''. God still loves them with a special love. We pray that they may recognize in Our Lord their own Messiah promised by God—and thus once more become part of the People of God, as they had been destined to be.

Like the Jews, the Moslems also believe in the one, true God. However, unlike Judaism, their religion is not the preparation for Christianity. The Moslem religion—Islam—developed in Arabia about six hundred years after Christ and draws from both Judaism and Christianity. They accept the revelation of God to the Jews found in the Old Testament but do not recognize Christ as the Messiah. They see him as one of the prophets, not as the Second Person of the Trinity. We pray that the Moslems, too, may see the truth and one day be fully united to the Church.

Almighty and eternal God, you created mankind so that all might long to find you and have peace when you are found. Grant that, in spite of hurtful things that stand in their way, they may all recognize in the lives of Christians the tokens of your love and mercy and gladly acknowledge you as the one true God and Father of us all (*General Intercession from the Liturgy of Good Friday*).

Then there are those people—both the *pagans* and the *atheists*—who do not believe in the one, true God at all. The pagans are those who do not believe in the only true God but may practice some form of idolatrous religion or even believe in many gods, which is called *polytheism*. The ancient Greek and Roman religions were of this sort. There are also those pagans who practice *animism*, believing that inanimate objects possess supernatural powers and can be controlled by us. The pagans then worship many gods, but not the one, true God.

There are also people who are *atheists*. Strictly speaking, atheism is the denial of the existence of a personal God. In our modern world atheism takes many forms. There are those who expressly deny God's existence. Others maintain that there may be a God but that we can know nothing about him. We call these people *agnostics*. Still other people do not expressly deny God's existence but never take any interest in God or religion. They choose to ignore him and concentrate on mankind and its accomplishments instead.

There can be many obstacles that prevent these people from believing in God. We pray that God will remove these obstacles, so they too may come to believe in him.

As members of the Church we should work toward the reunion of all Christians with the Church and pray that all others outside the Church might fully become members of the Mystical Body. This is what is meant by *ecumenism*. As Catholics we have been given a great gift, and we should have a longing to share this gift with others.

We know that salvation has come into the world through Christ. He left us the Church to distribute to us the graces of salvation and to provide a secure guide for us. We have been blessed with the sacraments that help us on our path to Heaven. Christ also left us with a visible representative on earth, so that we might

clearly see his message in the world. Those who are outside the Catholic Church do not have these great gifts. Does this mean, then, that those who are outside the visible Church cannot be saved?

The Church teaches that "outside the Catholic Church there is no salvation". What exactly does this mean? The Church is necessary for salvation because Jesus Christ is necessary for salvation. Jesus and his message are found completely in the Church—his Body.

The Church does not teach, however, that all of those who are outside the visible Church will not be saved. Only those who know that God wants them to be in full communion with the Catholic Church, yet who deliberately choose to remain outside the Church—by willingly rejecting Christ and his message—will not be saved. There are many people, though, who are outside the visible Church through no fault of their own. For example, there are many who have never heard the gospel or may have a distorted picture of it. If they live a good life, trying to do what God expects of them, they have hope of salvation.

But a problem still exists. Our Lord told us that Baptism *is* necessary in order to enter Heaven. When he spoke to the Pharisee Nicodemus, he said:

> Truly, truly I say to you, unless one is born of water and the Spirit, he cannot enter the Kingdom of God (Jn 3:5).

We have already seen that those Christians who are outside the Church are truly baptized in Christ, but what about those who have never been baptized—can they enter into the Kingdom of God?

For those who do not know of the sacrament and its importance, or who are unable to receive it before they die, there are two other means of receiving the sanctifying grace necessary to enter Heaven. The first is called *Baptism of desire*. This desire for Baptism can be explicit as in the case of someone who is preparing for Baptism but who dies before receiving the sacrament. Or it can be implicit. The desire is implied in those people who *faithfully* and *truly* try to carry out God's will in their lives. Perhaps they do not know of the need for Baptism but would receive it if they did. God, knowing their thoughts and desires, does not punish them for circumstances beyond their control.

The second extraordinary means of receiving the grace necessary for Heaven is called *Baptism of blood*. This is the "baptism" granted to those non-Christians who have been martyred for Christ. The fact that they are willing to die for Christ demonstrates their faith, and they

are welcomed into Heaven, although they have never received sacramental Baptism.

Now that we see the great gift we have been given by being baptized and raised as members of the Catholic Church, we should work to bring others into union with the Church. At the same time we should show respect for the religions of others, leading them with patience and compassion to see the truth.

We ought to see that we are unworthy to receive such a gift, and not think that this entitles us to feel smug and superior. Indeed we can learn from so many of our separated brethren.

The Eastern Orthodox venerate tradition. The splendor of their liturgy inspires in us deep reverence for the worship of God. Episcopalians have a great understanding for the beauty of ceremonies. Lutherans, Baptists, and Evangelicals read the Bible and are very familiar with it. Jews have a deep sense of the sacred, love the Commandments, and have the courage to stand up for their beliefs.

We Catholics must live our faith more seriously. Our love must increase, and each of us must personally convert, and turn away from sinful ways and follow Christ.

Words to Know:

separated brethren
chosen people   atheist   agnostic
ecumenism   animism   polytheism

Q. 26 *Can another Church, besides the Roman Catholic Church, be the Church of Jesus Christ, or at least part of it?*

No church, outside of the Roman Catholic Church, can be the Church of Jesus Christ, and not even part of it, because such a church cannot, like the Roman Catholic Church, have the singular and distinctive qualities of the Church of Christ, that is one, holy, Catholic and apostolic. As a matter of fact, none of the other churches which are called "Christian" have these distinctive qualities.

Q. 27 *Is it a serious loss to be outside the Church?*

It is a most serious loss to be outside the Church, because outside one does not have either the means which have been established or the secure guidance which has been set up for eternal salvation, which is the only thing truly necessary for man.

Q. 28 *Will a person outside the Church be saved?*

A person outside the Church by his own fault, and who dies without perfect contrition, will not be saved. But he who finds himself outside without fault of his own, and who lives a good life, can be saved by the love called charity, which unites unto God, and in a spiritual way also to the Church.

Church Teaching

"For although the Catholic Church has been endowed with all divinely revealed truth and with all means of grace, yet her members fail to live by them with all the fervor that they should. As a result the radiance of the Church's face shines less brightly in the eyes of our separated brethren and of the world at large, and the growth of God's Kingdom is retarded. Every Catholic must therefore aim at Christian perfection and, each according to his station, play his part, that the Church, which bears in her own body the humility and dying of Jesus, may daily be more purified and renewed, against the day when Christ will present her to himself in all her glory without spot or wrinkle" (UR, 4).

PART TWO

The Christian In the World

CHAPTER 14

The Universal Call to Holiness

". . . but as he who called you is holy, be holy yourselves in all your conduct: since it is written 'you shall be holy, for I am holy' " (1 Pet 1:15—16).

As members of the Mystical Body we have a general calling, or *vocation*, from God. Each Christian is called to *holiness*, which means that we are each called to follow Christ so that one day we may be with him in Heaven for eternity. As St. Paul tells us in his letter to the Christians in Ephesus, God "chose us in him before the foundation of the world, that we should be holy and blameless before him" (Eph 1:4). The vocation of each Christian, then, is to become a saint.

In addition to becoming saints, we are also called by God to spread the faith given at our Baptism. Each of us must be a missionary, or apostle, for Christ, preaching the gospel in whatever way we can, by word and by example. We call this work the *apostolate*.

For each of us, becoming a saint and spreading the faith are done in different ways. This is our *specific vocation*, to which God calls us, according to our own gifts, talents, and circumstances. St. Paul, in his letter to the Romans, reminds us that the Church, like the body, has many members, each of which has its own particular role:

Having gifts that differ according to the grace given to us, let us use them: if prophecy, in proportion to our faith; if service, in our serving; he who teaches, in his teaching; he who exhorts, in his exhortation; he who contributes, in liberality; he who gives aid, with zeal; he who does acts of mercy, with cheerfulness (Rom 12:6—8).

Thus our own particular vocation depends upon the gifts that God has given us.

In discovering our vocation, we cannot simply follow our own desires, for often these may lead us away from God. Nor can we expect God to hand us a detailed list of instructions about how to live our lives. Rather, we should pray for the wisdom to recognize our talents and abilities—as well as our limitations—and to choose our life's work accordingly. We also have to recognize the circumstances we are in, where God has placed us. For instance, a father who has to take care of his family cannot say, "Well, I have a special gift to be an artist [or some other talent], so I ought to pursue that instead of the drudgery of my job or of the care of my children." In later chapters we will consider the possible states of life to which God may call us.

Obstacles to Holiness

Before considering how to become holy, we shall look first at those things that are obstacles to holiness. We know that all men are born with original sin, and that it is removed through Baptism. After Baptism, however, we are still weak and inclined toward sin. We are still easily tempted, and inclined toward evil, toward disobedience to God and his Commandments.

This inclination to sin can also be seen in the way we often use our natural tendencies. God has placed in all men certain tendencies to help us live here on earth. For example, we have a natural desire for food and drink so that we can survive physically. Because of original sin it is easy for these tendencies to get out of control. When this occurs, they lead us to sin. For example, the desire for food and drink can become excessive, leading a person to gluttony or drunkenness.

If we allow these tendencies to get out of control frequently, they can become *habits*. Habits are ways of acting that are acquired by repetition of certain actions. Habits are a familiar part of our daily routine. We brush our teeth, for example, without giving it much thought. Once we have learned to ride a bi- cycle, we develop the habit and ride without thinking about all the steps we are following. These habits are morally indifferent—that is, they are neither good nor evil. Some habits, however, are sinful. These are acquired by repeatedly doing bad actions and are known as vices.

There are seven principal vices, which are known as the seven *capital sins*. They are called *capital*, from the Latin word for head or source, because they are the source of all other sins and vices. They are not the only vices, just the chief ones from which many more stem. Because these vices are the major obstacles in our path to holiness, we should consider each of them briefly and learn to recognize them.

> *"The beginning of man's pride is to depart from the Lord; . . . for the beginning of pride is to sin, and the man who clings to it pours out abominations"* (Sir 10:14—15).

Pride is the chief capital sin, for it is at the root of all the others. It is an *excessive*, *disordered* love of oneself. This leads us to prefer our own desires to those of God and our neighbors. It is pride that was at the root of the sin of our first parents—their desire to be like God.

Church Teaching

"It is therefore quite clear that all Christians in any state or walk of life are called to the fullness of Christian life and to the perfection of love, and by this holiness a more human manner of life is fostered also in earthly society. In order to reach this perfection the faithful should use the strength dealt out to them by Christ's gift, so that, following in his footsteps and conformed to his image, doing the will of God in everything, they may wholeheartedly devote themselves to the glory of God and to the service of their neighbor" (LG, 40).

They did not want to be subordinate, as creatures, to their Creator. We should not confuse this vice with the rightful pride we take in our accomplishments or with a correct sense of self-esteem. These are sinful only if we exaggerate them.

"And [Jesus] said to them, 'Take heed, and beware of all covetousness; for a man's life does not consist in the abundance of his possessions' " (Lk 12:15).

Covetousness, or avarice, means greed. It is an uncontrolled desire for earthly possessions, such as money, clothes, and so on. A certain desire for these things is natural, since they are necessary in order to live in the world. However, we must constantly take care that these desires do not turn to greed, and that we do not put these things first in our lives or ahead of more important values. Not only is covetousness itself wrong, as the Ninth and Tenth Commandments tell us, but greed can easily lead to further sins. For example, the person with this vice may eventually lie, cheat, steal, or even murder, in order to possess those things he desires.

"But I say, walk by the Spirit, and do not gratify the desires of the flesh. For the desires of the flesh are against the Spirit, and the desires of the Spirit are against the flesh; . . . Now the works of the flesh are plain: immorality, impurity, licentiousness" (Gal 5:16—19).

Lust is the uncontrolled desire for or indulgence in sexual pleasure. It should not be confused with the lawful use of our sexual powers within the holy state of marriage. God created human beings with a natural attraction to the opposite sex. As long as this attraction is controlled and ordered finally to Christian marriage, it is healthy and good. This attraction becomes disordered when it is focused on our own pleasure instead of a selfless, true love of another person, and when it is separated from marriage and the purpose of marriage.

"Be angry but do not sin; do not let the sun go down on your anger. . . . Let all bitterness and wrath and anger and clamor and slander be put away from you" (Eph 4:26, 31).

Anger is an uncontrolled expression of displeasure and antagonism, often accompanied by a desire for revenge. This is not the same as the righteous anger spoken of by St. Paul in his letter to the Ephesians or that exhibited by Our Lord when he threw the moneychangers out of the Temple. Anger is the proper response to an injustice—for example, defrauding the poor, abortion—but we must control it and use it properly. If our anger is uncontrolled or if it is bitter and full of hate and we seek only revenge, it has become a vice.

"Let your light so shine before men, that they may see your good works and give glory to your Father who is in Heaven."

(Matthew 5:16)

"Do not have an insatiable appetite for any luxury, and do not give yourself up to food; . . . Many have died of gluttony, but he who is careful to avoid it prolongs his life" (Sir 37:29–31).

Gluttony is an uncontrolled desire for and indulgence in food and drink. Eating and drinking are intended to be pleasurable and are certainly not sinful in themselves. In fact, they are necessary for our survival. However, like our desire for possessions, these desires can become excessive and be abused by us.

"For where jealousy [envy] and selfish ambition exist, there will be disorder and every vile practice" (James 3:16).

Envy is unhappiness or discontent over the good fortune or success of others. We are envious when we are saddened at another's prosperity or when we rejoice in another's misfortune. This vice is not the same as the ordinary desire or wish we might have to be successful like someone else. Similarly, it is not the wish or desire to possess a certain talent.

"And whatever you do, in word or deed, do everything in the name of the Lord Jesus, giving thanks to God the Father through him."

(Colossians 3:17)

"And we desire each one of you to show the same earnestness in realizing the full assurance of hope until the end, so that you may not be sluggish, but imitators of those who through faith and patience inherit the promises" (Heb 6:11–12).

Sloth is excessive laziness or carelessness. It is unlike the other vices, because it is not an ordinary desire that is uncontrolled. It is really a lack of desire to do one's duties, particularly spiritual ones, because of the effort that is involved. It is not the same as a reasonable desire for times of rest or leisure.

We do not all have equal inclinations to these vices. Some of us must struggle more against temptations to envy, while others are more tempted by anger or gluttony. The first step on the path to holiness is to look at ourselves, try to recognize our weaknesses, and try to overcome them with God's help.

In the next chapter we will consider positive steps to holiness. We will study the virtues, what they are and how we can develop them.

Words to Know:

vocation   apostolate
habit   capital sins

Q. 29 *What is a vice?*

A vice is a habit of doing evil, acquired by repeating bad actions.

Q. 30 *What are the principal vices?*

The principal vices are the seven capital sins. They are given this name because they are the source and the origin of other vices and sins.

Q. 31 *What are the virtues opposed to the capital sins?*

The virtues opposed to the capital sins are humility, liberality, chastity, patience, sobriety, brotherliness, and diligence in the service of God.

Prayer

"Almighty and eternal God, your Spirit guides the Church and makes it holy. Listen to our prayers and help each of us in his vocation to do your work more faithfully. We ask this through Christ Our Lord. *Amen*."

(General Intercessions, Holy Week)

CHAPTER 15

The Life of Virtue

"He has showed you, O man, what is good; and what does the Lord require of you but to do justice, and to love kindness, and to walk humbly with your God?" (Micah 6:8).

Just as there are habits that can be obstacles to our pursuit of holiness, there are also habits that can help us. If we consciously and willingly perform a good action frequently, we will be on the right path and acquire a disposition to do it again. Then it becomes more and more part of us. It takes root in us. For example, if we tell the truth, or perform one generous act, we have not yet acquired the virtue of honesty or generosity. But if we repeat it we will be strengthened. The word *virtue* comes from the Latin word for strength.

A virtue is an abiding disposition of the soul, or power that enables a person to perform good actions easily and to avoid bad actions. It can be either *natural*—that is, acquired through repeated action, such as the virtue of honesty—or *supernatural*, that is, given to us by God.

The natural virtues in many ways resemble other habits. Take the example of a runner. At first running is difficult and a big effort for him. He endures and overcomes obstacles. Finally he can easily run for miles. He has the strength to do it. And then he even loves running.

So it is with virtues. We make the effort. We conquer the obstacles, and then we grow stronger, it becomes easier, and we finally love it. It is a joy for us. We conquer sin and grow closer to God. (Sinful habits give us, for a moment of pleasure, unhappiness and a feeling of sadness in the end.) St. Benedict says that as we progress in virtue "our hearts shall be enlarged, and we shall run with unspeakable sweetness of love in the way of God's commandments."

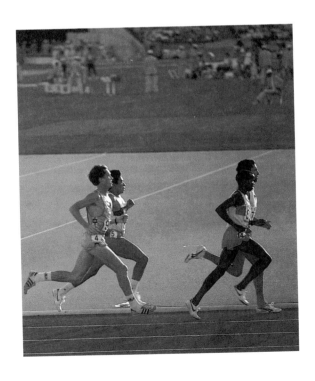

And if one loves righteousness her labors are virtues; for she teaches self-control and prudence, justice and courage; nothing in life is more profitable for men than these (Wis 8:7).

The Cardinal Virtues

The natural, or *moral*, virtues enable us to act rightly in our conduct with other men. The chief moral virtues are the four *cardinal* virtues. They are called cardinal, from the Latin word for hinge, because they are the support or framework for all the other moral virtues. These four—prudence, justice, temperance (self-control), and fortitude (courage)—are the foundation for living a good life.

Prudence is the chief moral virtue, which directs all the others. Also called practical wisdom, this virtue enables us to determine what action is required in a given situation, and it moves us to do the action. The person who acts using good judgment at all times—knowing the right thing to do in every situation—has the virtue of prudence. Prudence requires that we know what to do and that we have the will to do it.

Prudence should be operating in all the decisions we make in our lives. We must learn to examine a situation clearly and to decide on the proper course of action with deliberation. For this to become a habit takes time and a great deal of experience.

Justice is the virtue that prompts us to give to others what is due to them—that is, what they deserve. Justice prompts us to pay debts owed to another, to keep promises that we have made, to obey laws made by those who have the authority, to keep secrets that someone entrusts to us, to play games fairly, and to respect the property of others. Justice directs us to act fairly and honestly toward others; it is commanded by the Seventh Commandment.

For those in authority, acting justly sometimes means assigning punishments, since at times they may be deserved.

There are some debts that we can never fully repay—for example, the debts we owe to God who created us, to our parents for giving us life and raising us, or to our country. The respect, love, and loyalty that we show to them are derived from this virtue of justice.

Fortitude is the virtue that enables us to confront difficulties or dangers, perhaps even death, with courage and hope. With fortitude we are able to act calmly and reasonably even in the face of great dangers.

The martyrs of the Church all demonstrated the virtue of fortitude when they chose to remain faithful to Christ, despite the terrible deaths that awaited them. We might never be called upon to die for Christ, yet we need to develop the virtue of fortitude to be able to face the difficult moments in our lives—perhaps refusing to get drunk or use drugs when others encourage us to do this. St. Paul exhorts us to practice the virtue of fortitude when he says, in his letter to the Ephesians:

Take the whole armor of God, that you may be able to withstand in the evil day, and having done all, to stand (Eph 6:13).

Temperance is the virtue that enables us to control our passions and desires. This virtue allows us to act moderately and reasonably, so that we may use our bodies correctly. We often think of temperance as applying particularly to food and drink. This is true, but it also applies to all areas of our lives. The temperate person is one who eats the right amount, exercises the right amount, sleeps the right amount, and so on—that is, he is a person who habitually balances all activities of life.

Upon these four virtues hang many other moral virtues. One of these is the virtue of *religion*. Religion is the virtue by which we give to God the worship he deserves. This means that we praise him in a manner that is appropriate to his place as our Creator and Lord. This virtue stems from the cardinal virtue of justice.

Other Moral Virtues

Other moral virtues stemming from the cardinal virtues help us to counteract the seven capital sins. These good habits will replace the bad habits that can so easily develop.

Humility is the virtue opposed to pride. It leads one to have a just opinion of one's self and to give credit for our successes and gifts to God. Humility is related to the virtue of prudence, because it enables us to see the correct way to think about ourselves.

Liberality is the virtue opposed to covetousness. It enables a person to give freely of his money, possessions, talents, and so on to worthy purposes. Stemming from justice, liberality enables one to act fairly with his gifts and to serve the needs of others.

Chastity is the virtue opposed to lust. Chastity should not be seen *only* as self-control, moderation, and balance of sexual inclinations, but more importantly it should be understood in relation to the expression of human love. What does this mean? It means that sex is a great gift which by its nature entails complete donation of one person to another only in marriage. It therefore means abstaining from sex outside of marriage, so that the purest love can be given most completely to the spouse, or, in the case of priests and religious, to God in loving abstinence.

Meekness is the virtue opposed to anger. It is the virtue that enables us to be patient under injury or insult. The meek person is able to control his temper even in a trying or difficult situation. Because this takes a certain amount of spiritual strength or courage, meekness is related to the virtue of fortitude.

Moderation and *sobriety* are virtues opposed to gluttony. They enable one to use food and drink sensibly—enjoying them in the proper amounts and at suitable times. As forms of self-control, they stem from the cardinal virtue of temperance.

Brotherly love is the virtue opposed to envy. This virtue enables one to show true love for one's neighbor—praying for him, doing acts of kindness for him, and helping him in his needs. This virtue stems from the virtue of justice—for we are giving to another what is owed.

Diligence is the virtue opposed to sloth. This virtue enables us to do our work and carry out our religious duties—whatever they may be—with devotion and dedication. It stems from the virtue of prudence, for we see that hard work at our given tasks is the right way to act.

Discussion Question: There are many more virtues that hang on the cardinal virtues—such as honesty, courtesy, loyalty, and so on. What other virtues can you think of? To which cardinal virtues are they related?

The Theological Virtues

The supernatural virtues are those that belong to us as Christians. Unlike the moral virtues, they cannot be acquired by repetition of certain actions, but are *infused*, given to us, by God. We receive them at Baptism, when we receive sanctifying grace. We exercise these virtues with the help of God, through the actual graces he gives us.

The supernatural virtues are faith, hope, and charity. Because these virtues come from God as well as direct us toward him, they are called *theological* virtues (theological in this sense means pertaining to God).

Faith is the virtue by which we believe all that God has revealed to us through Christ and his Church. The gift of faith is necessary, for it enables us to believe those mysteries—such as the Trinity—that are beyond the grasp of the human mind. We need faith in order to know our goal, which is Heaven.

Hope is the virtue by which we trust in God's promises of eternal salvation. With hope we can find comfort in the words of Our Lord: "I am the resurrection and the life: whoever believes in me, though he should die, will come to life" (Jn 11:25—26). Hope tells us that God, who promised us eternal salvation, will also give us the graces that we need to reach Heaven.

Charity is the virtue by which we love God above all things for his own sake and love our neighbor as ourselves. The two Great Commandments of which Our Lord spoke to the scribe (Lk 10:25—28) can be summed up in the virtue of charity. This virtue enables us to love God above all, simply because he is good and deserves our love. We love our neighbors,

including our enemies, because God loves them and because they, like ourselves, have been created in his image.

> So faith, hope, love abide, these three, but the greatest of these is love (1 Cor 13:13).

All three of these virtues are necessary if we are to reach Heaven, but charity, which is love in its highest and fullest sense, is the greatest. It is the virtue that unites us most intimately with God and our neighbor. It is through charity that we are moved to obey God's law and to perform good actions. Every virtue we have studied so far becomes radiant, beautiful, and new when infused by this love. As St. Paul says, all things are made new through Jesus Christ (see 2 Cor 5:17).

While the theological virtues cannot be acquired through repetition of certain acts, we can strengthen them by our actions. Through prayer we open ourselves to God's grace so that we can receive these great gifts. If we *really* want them and *really* strive after them, then we will receive them. Christ says, "Ask and you shall receive, . . . knock and it shall be opened to you" (Mt 7:7). Just as our bodies require exercise to remain in shape, so these virtues must be exercised if they are to help us reach Heaven. In general, we can develop and exercise these virtues by making acts of faith, hope, and charity.

Faith is strengthened when we profess and defend our faith, and when we study and think about the meaning of the mysteries of the faith. It is also made stronger by the good actions that we do, since ". . . faith apart from works is dead" (James 2:26). We can exercise hope by accepting the will of God, trusting him to care for us as he cares for the birds of the air and the lilies of the field (Lk 12:22—34). By doing so we can avoid becoming unduly anxious or upset by life—even by trials or sorrows. We strengthen the virtue of charity by observing the Commandments, as Our Lord instructed us: "He who hears my Commandments and keeps them, he it is who loves me. . . . If a man loves me, he will keep my word" (Jn 14:21, 23). We also exercise charity by doing the works of mercy, which we will consider in the next chapter.

Living the virtuous life—practicing these virtues daily—is not easy. It is, in fact, a great challenge. But it is a challenge that we can meet, because we have God's help through prayer and the sacraments. In our struggle we should remember the saints. They are the proof for us that the life of virtue is possible. They also show that virtue will be rewarded by God.

Finally, we should recall the example of Our Lord himself. Christ is both God and man. But he showed us as man the perfect way to live as a human being.

Words to Know:

   virtue   cardinal virtue

Q. 32   *What is a virtue?*

A virtue is an abiding disposition of the soul to do good.

Q. 33   *How many kinds of virtues are there?*

There are two kinds of virtues. First, the natural virtues, which we acquire by repeating naturally good acts. These are called moral virtues of the natural order. Secondly, the supernatural virtues, which we cannot acquire or even exercise by our own powers for they come to us as gifts from God and are the virtues proper to the Christian.

Q. 34   *What are the virtues proper to the Christian?*

The virtues proper to the Christian are the supernatural virtues, and in particular, *faith*, *hope*, and *charity*. These last three are called the *theological* or divine virtues, because they have God himself for their object and their motive.

Q. 35   *How do we receive and exercise these supernatural virtues?*

We receive these supernatural virtues together with sanctifying grace, by means of the sacraments or by perfect charity. We exercise them with the help of actual graces, namely, the good thoughts and inspirations with which God moves and helps us in every good act that we do.

Q. 36 *Which is the most excellent among the supernatural virtues?*

The most excellent among the supernatural virtues is charity, because it is inseparable from sanctifying grace, because it unites us intimately to God and to our neighbor, because it moves us to perfect observation of the law and to do every good work, and finally because it will carry on into the life to come. Thus Christian perfection consists in charity.

Q. 37 *What is faith?*

Faith is the supernatural virtue by which we believe, on the authority of God, what he has revealed and proposes to us for belief by means of the Church.

Q. 38 *Where do we find preserved what God has revealed and proposes for our belief by means of the Church?*

That which God has revealed and proposes to us for belief by means of the Church is preserved in *Sacred Scripture* and in *Tradition*.

Q. 39 *Who can bring us with authority to know, completely and in their true sense, the truths contained in Scripture and Tradition?*

The Church alone can bring us with authority to know the truths contained in Scripture and Tradition, completely, and in their true sense, because God has entrusted the deposit of faith to the Church and has sent the Holy Spirit upon the Church. The Holy Spirit continually assists the Church so that she makes no error in carrying out this assignment.

Q. 40 *Is it sufficient to believe the truths revealed by God?*

It is not sufficient to believe the truths revealed by God in a general way; certain ones of them, namely, the existence of God, who rewards the good and punishes the evil, and the two chief mysteries of the faith, must be believed with an explicit act of faith.

Q. 41 *What is hope?*

Hope is the supernatural virtue by which we trust in God and expect to receive from him eternal life and the graces necessary to merit this eternal life by our good works here on earth.

Q. 42 *What is the reason why we hope to receive eternal life from God and the graces necessary to merit it?*

We hope to receive eternal life and the graces necessary to merit it from God because he who is infinitely good and faithful has promised it to us through the merits of Jesus Christ. Therefore, whoever distrusts God or despairs of his own salvation, offends God in the highest degree.

Q. 43 *What is charity?*

Charity is the supernatural virtue by which we love God for his own sake above every other thing, and our neighbor as ourselves for the love of God.

Q. 44 *Why must we love God?*

We must love God for his own sake because he is supremely good, the source of every good thing that we have. Therefore we must also love him above every other thing "with all our heart, with all our soul, with all our mind, and with all our strength" (Mk 12:30).

Q. 45 *Why must we love our neighbor?*

We must love our neighbor for the love of God because God commands it and because every human being has been created in the image of God, like ourselves, and hence is our brother.

Q. 46 *Are we obliged also to love our enemies?*

Yes, we are obliged also to love our enemies, forgiving the offenses we may have received, because our enemies are also our neighbors and because Jesus Christ has given us explicit command to love our enemies.

Q. 47 *Is it good to make frequent acts of faith, hope, and charity?*

Yes, it is indeed good to make acts of faith, hope, and charity frequently, in order to preserve, to increase, and to strengthen these virtues which are so necessary to us, for they are as it were the living parts of the "spiritual man".

Q. 48 *How should we make acts of faith, hope, and charity?*

We should make acts of faith, hope, and charity with our heart, with our lips, and *with the things that we do*, giving proof of them in our behavior.

Q. 49 *How do we give proof of our faith?*

We give proof of our faith by professing it and defending it, when need arises, without fear and without human respect. We also give proof of our faith by living according to its teachings: "Faith without works is dead" (James 2:26).

Q. 50 *How do we give proof of hope?*

We give proof of our hope by not letting ourselves become disturbed by the wretchedness and contradictions of life, and not even by persecutions; but by living in peaceful resignation to Providence, secure in the promises of God.

Q. 51 *How do we prove our charity?*

We prove our charity by observing the Commandments of God, by practicing the works of mercy, and, if God calls us to it, by following the evangelical counsels.

Q. 52 *What is a moral virtue?*

A moral virtue is a habit of doing good, acquired by repeatedly doing good acts.

Q. 53 *What are the principal moral virtues?*

The principal moral virtues are religion, which brings us to give God the worship owing to him, and the four cardinal virtues: prudence, justice, fortitude, and temperance, which bring us to live in an upright way.

Q. 54 *Why are these virtues called cardinal virtues?*

These virtues are called cardinal because they are the "hinges", as it were, or the support of all the other moral virtues.

Q. 55 *What is prudence?*

Prudence is the virtue which directs our actions to the right kind of purpose, and gives us the ability to discern and to use right means for attaining that purpose.

Q. 56 *What is justice?*

Justice is the virtue which brings us to give each one what is due to him.

Q. 57 *What is fortitude?*

Fortitude is the virtue which brings us to confront without temerity or fear any difficulty or danger, even death itself, for the service of God and the welfare of our neighbor.

Q. 58 *What is temperance?*

Temperance is the virtue which holds under control our passions and desires, especially the sensual ones, and which brings us to moderation in using goods of the senses.

Q. 59 *What are the passions?*

The passions are violent movements or impulses of the soul which, if they are not moderated by our reason, lead us to vice, and often also to sin itself.

CHAPTER 16

The Works of Mercy And Happiness

"Then the just will ask him: 'Lord, when did we see you hungry and feed you or see you thirsty and give you drink? When did we welcome you away from home or clothe you in your nakedness? When did we visit you when you were ill or in prison?' The king will answer them: 'I assure you, as often as you did it for one of my least brothers, you did it for me'" (Mt 25:37–40).

We grow in virtue, particularly in practicing the *works of mercy*. In these acts we show our love for Christ by helping our neighbor. Our Lord told us, "Truly, I say to you, as you did it to one of the least of these my brethren, you did it to me" (Mt 25:40).

Since we have both bodies and souls—and both require care—the works of mercy are divided into two groups. We care for our neighbors' souls and spiritual needs through the *spiritual works of mercy*. We care for their bodies and physical needs through *corporal works of mercy* (the Latin word *corpus* means "body").

Because our souls are the most important part of our human nature—the part by which we can think, know, and freely choose good or evil—the seven spiritual works of mercy are the most important. As we consider each of

them, think of how you can practice these in your life. Remember that the heart and soul of each of these works is love; love is their moving force.

Spiritual Works

Admonish the sinner. Because sin separates one from God, it is truly an act of love to help another person realize the seriousness of sin and the need for forgiveness. This does not mean humiliating someone in public or acting as if we ourselves have never sinned. Rather, we should quietly and tactfully steer our friends away from occasions of sin or encourage those who have sinned to seek forgiveness in the sacrament of Penance, giving them hope that they will be able to overcome sinful ways with the mercy of God.

Instruct the ignorant. Helping a person to learn or understand the truths that God has revealed to us is a second way to nourish another's spiritual life. Our religion teachers and parents, of course, do this for us, but there are also other ways to practice this work of mercy as well. There are many people who have not heard the message of the gospel in its fullness. We can often find opportunities to tell them about it, remembering the words of Our Lord:

No one after lighting a lamp puts it in a cellar or under a bushel, but on a stand, that those who enter may see the light (Lk 11:33).

We have been given the "light of faith" and should not hide it but should let it shine forth. However, we must avoid preaching or acting as if we know all the answers.

Counsel the doubtful. To counsel someone means giving him advice or guidance. Those who most need this counsel are people who are weak in the virtues of faith and hope. For example, someone may reject certain beliefs of the faith—or at least question them—or may fall into despair, doubting that God will forgive him for his sins. These people need loving guidance and encouragement to strengthen them, thus bringing them closer to God once more.

Comfort the sorrowful. Suffering is a part of our life in this world. Indeed, Our Lord told us that those who wish to follow him must first take up their cross, just as he took up his Cross for us. Each of us has our own specific crosses that Our Lord asks us to bear out of love for him. This is not always easy, and this work of mercy reminds us that we should help one another to bear the sufferings in our lives. Sometimes a word of love and understanding can help. Sometimes a kind deed can lighten the burden of someone else's suffering.

Bear wrongs patiently. It is important to remember that it is better to suffer an injustice than to be guilty of committing one ourselves. In his Sermon on the Mount, Our Lord said:

I say to you. . . . Love your enemies, do good to those who hate you, bless those who curse you, pray for those who abuse you. To him who strikes you on the cheek, offer the other also; and from him who takes away your cloak do not withhold your coat as well (Lk 6:27–29).

This true charity is the mark of the Christian, and we must learn to be patient and strong when we are the victims of injustice. It is by such actions that we may draw others to Christ.

Forgive all injuries. Not only must we patiently bear these wrongs, we must also forgive those who injure us. In the *Lord's Prayer*, which Jesus taught us, we say, "Forgive us our trespasses, as we forgive those who trespass against us" (see Mt 6:12). This means the measure by which we forgive will be the measure by which God will forgive us. By forgiving others we imitate the love that Christ shows for us. He offers forgiveness to all—even those who put him to death on the Cross.

Pray for the living and the dead. We have already seen that the Communion of Saints means that we can pray for one another. This act of love is one of the easiest—and one of the most important—ways to help others. We recall that charity toward our neighbor includes our enemies, and our prayers should extend to them as well. When we pray for those who have died, let us remember not only our relatives and friends, but also those souls who are most forgotten.

Discussion Question: What are some specific ways that you, as eighth-graders, can practice these spiritual works of mercy?

Corporal Works

The seven corporal works of mercy are those acts of love that Our Lord spoke about when he described the Last Judgment. To those who practice these works Our Lord will say:

Come, O blessed of my Father, inherit the Kingdom prepared for you from the foundation of the world; for I was hungry and you gave me food; I was thirsty and you gave me drink; I was a stranger and you welcomed me; I was naked and you clothed me; I was sick and you visited me; I was in prison and you came to me (Mt 25:34–36).

Feed the hungry, give drink to the thirsty, and clothe the naked. Most of us have been greatly blessed by God. Nevertheless, there are many people in the world—even some in our country—who lack many of the basic needs of life. We must not neglect these people. It is an obligation of charity to help them. While we may not be able to help these people directly or dramatically, we can contribute money or possessions to groups whose works are such charitable activities. For example, there may be an organization in your parish—such as the St. Vincent de Paul Society—which carries out these works of mercy.

These works of mercy start in the family. Parents are responsible for seeing that their children are fed and clothed. In the same way, when the children are older they are responsible for taking care of these needs for their aging parents. At this point in our lives we can practice these works of mercy in simple ways. For example, we can prepare lunch for a hungry brother or sister or share some of our clothes with others in our family. Families together can reach out to other poorer families. These acts of mercy will prepare us for greater works as we grow older.

Visit the imprisoned. There are many kinds of people in prison. There is the hardened criminal. Some great conversions have taken place among the most hardened, and perhaps the grace they received came through the prayers

The Spiritual Works of Mercy	The Corporal Works of Mercy
Admonish the sinner Instruct the ignorant Counsel the doubtful Comfort the sorrowful Bear wrongs patiently Forgive all injuries Pray for the living and the dead	Feed the hungry Give drink to the thirsty Clothe the naked Visit the imprisoned Shelter the homeless Visit the sick Bury the dead

or kindness of people who knew them. There are some who were weak and made mistakes but are now sorry for what they have done. These need to be encouraged, so that they will continue to reform their lives. Some are innocent. If we are able, we should help them obtain justice. In the meantime, they need our moral support.

There are still other people who are not in jail, but whose state in life can be like a prison—separating them from other people and the support such contact brings. For example, some who, for a long period of time, must care for a sick relative at home may need our visits to help him accept his present cross.

Shelter the homeless. There are many homeless people in our cities. We should pay attention to their great need. For example, Trevor Ferrell, a twelve-year-old boy in Philadelphia brought the street people blankets from his own home. The word got around and soon the whole neighborhood was helping. Finally they even rented a house for the homeless. We may not always be able to do much directly for those people who are homeless. However, we can practice this work of mercy by being will-

ing to share our homes with someone in need —for example, a friend whose home has been damaged by a fire or flood. We can also willingly share our own room with a brother or sister if this is needed in our family.

Visit the sick. The sick are often frightened and may be in particular need of encouragement. It is not always easy for us who are healthy to understand the suffering sick people go through. Visiting them may give them the strength they need to bear their cross. Perhaps they may need us in some practical way. Christ can touch them through our acts of love.

Bury the dead. The final act of mercy is mentioned in the Old Testament. The angel Raphael praised Tobias for this charitable act:

> And when you buried the dead, I was likewise present with you. When you did not hesitate to rise and leave your dinner in order to go and lay out the dead, your good deed was not hidden from me (Tob 12:13).

By this action we show respect for the body, because it is part of the human being. We can practice this work of mercy by attending a funeral of someone we knew—and offering consolation to those who are bereaved—or by respecting cemeteries, perhaps leaving flowers at the grave site of a relative.

By living the virtuous life and practicing the works of mercy, we will be *happy* for ever with God in Heaven. This is the happiness of which Our Lord spoke in the Sermon on the Mount (Mt 5:3—11). He promised this happiness to those who live the Christian life, which he summarized in the eight *Beatitudes*.

"Beatify" means "to make happy". A beatitude is a special happiness or blessing of a spiritual nature. These eight Beatitudes are the promises for happiness that Christ makes to those who faithfully accept his teaching and follow his example.

The happiness of which Our Lord speaks, however, is not what the world identifies with happiness—money, power, fame, and so on. Even when such things bring us pleasure or happiness, it is fleeting. The happiness that belongs to the *meek*, the *pure in heart*, and so on is the lasting happiness of eternal life. This happiness brings us true joy and peace even in our life on earth. It is the happiness which no one can take from us. It lasts for ever.

Words to Know:

> corporal works of mercy
> spiritual works of mercy

Q. 60 *Did Jesus Christ recommend to us any particular moral virtues?*
Jesus Christ recommended certain moral virtues in a particular way, included in the eight evangelical beatitudes, calling him happy and blessed who puts them in practice.

Q. 61 *Why does Jesus Christ in the evangelical beatitudes, contrary to the opinion of the world, call persons happy who are humble and who suffer tribulation?*
Jesus Christ, contrary to the opinion of the world, calls persons who are humble and who suffer tribulations "happy" because they will have a special reward from God; and he teaches us to imitate them, without paying attention to the deceitful maxims of the world.

Q. 62 *Can they be truly happy who follow the maxims of the world?*
They who follow the maxims of the world cannot be truly happy, because they do not seek God, their Lord and their true happiness; for this reason, they do not have peace of conscience, and they are on the way toward damnation.

CHAPTER 17

Vocations: The Religious Life And the Priesthood

"Under the impulse of love, which the Holy Spirit pours into their hearts, they live more and more for Christ and for his Body, the Church. The more fervently, therefore, they join themselves to Christ by this gift of their whole life, the fuller does the Church's life become and the more vigorous and fruitful its apostolate" (PC, 1).

In an earlier chapter we spoke of the vocation that all of us share as Christians—to follow Christ and ultimately to be with God in Heaven. Yet, each must pursue this goal differently, according to his own temperament and particular call from God. The vocation of most Christians is the life of a layman or laywoman in the world. For others, though, it will be the priestly or religious life.

We have seen that, from the beginning of Christianity, some in the Church have directly consecrated their lives to God by a vow. Although not everyone is called to this life, Our Lord invites many to follow him in this way. In the Gospels he tells us of the reward that will be given to those who answer this call:

And every one who has left houses or brothers or sisters or father or mother or children or lands for my name's sake, will receive a hundredfold, and inherit eternal life (Mt 19:29).

The call to the priesthood or the religious life is a vocation to follow Christ most perfectly on earth. Once Our Lord was approached by a rich, young man who asked what he must do to have eternal life. Our Lord told him:

"If you would enter life, keep the Commandments. . . ." The young man said to him, "All these I have observed; what do I still lack?" Jesus said to him, "If you would be *perfect*, go, sell what you possess and give to the poor, and you will have treasure in Heaven; and come, follow me" (Mt 19:17, 20–21).

Here Jesus was speaking of the call to the religious life—following the counsels of perfection.

Although this vocation is the highest call, God does not intend everyone to live the religious life. Each of us must seek holiness in the state that God wants us to live. The consecrated life calls for great generosity. Objectively, religious life is the most perfect. This does not mean that a lay person cannot attain perfection. Every vocation leads to holiness. Everyone must try to find out what God calls him to.

Religious Life

The religious life consists in following the three *evangelical counsels*, also known as the counsels of perfection. These are recommendations for perfect love taught and practiced by Christ—poverty, chastity, and obedience. Those who follow these counsels take *vows* (free, deliberate promises made to God) to keep each one. They willingly give up certain good things of this life—money and possessions, marriage, and liberty—in order to devote themselves more completely to loving and serving God and neighbor. These vows set a person free from temporal goods, so that he may freely give himself to love of God and neighbor.

The first counsel is poverty. The person who takes this vow gives up his earthly possessions in order to follow Christ. In our modern world, where so much emphasis is placed upon jobs, money, and possessions, this is indeed a sacrifice, even for one who is not rich.

Through religious life Christ calls for a life of total consecration in individual service to God and to one's neighbor. This means that you give to God the highest natural goods. One of these is the loving union with another person in marriage and family life. Human love in marriage is a holy thing, which Our Lord has blessed. Thus the sacrifice involved in giving this up is truly great. By the vow of chastity a

person consecrates himself more completely to God, surrendering the good of marriage.

Since one might fulfill the counsels of poverty and chastity but still be filled with love of self, God asks one final sacrifice of the person who dedicates his life to him. He asks that one surrender his own personal preferences and wishes. This is the vow of obedience. The person who follows this path then gives up his liberty, submitting himself completely through

''Father, in your plan for our salvation you provide shepherds for your people. Fill your Church with the spirit of courage and love. Raise up worthy ministers for your altars and ardent but gentle servants of the gospel. Grant this through Our Lord Jesus Christ, your Son, who lives and reigns with you and the Holy Spirit, one God, for ever and ever. *Amen*.''

(Sacramentary, Mass for Priestly Vocations)

"If you wish to be perfect, go and sell what you own and give the money to the poor, and you will have treasure in Heaven; then come, follow me."

(Matthew 19:21)

his legitimate religious superiors, to the will of God as it is manifest in the Church.

One who enters the religious life, practicing the vows of poverty, chastity, and obedience, does so in imitation of Christ himself. At his death Our Lord had nothing; the soldiers even cast lots for the clothes he had been wearing (Mt 27:35). At one time he said of himself, ". . . the Son of man has nowhere to lay his head" (Mt 8:20). We know Our Lord never married; he spent his public life preaching and teaching the Good News. Most important, he submitted his will to his Father in Heaven. This was particularly demonstrated on the eve of his death, when he prayed in the Garden of Gethsemane. Knowing what lay ahead of him, he said:

> Father, if thou art willing, remove this cup from me: nevertheless not my will, but thine, be done (Lk 22:42).

Those in the religious life are an example to all people. They remind us of the importance of placing God first in our lives. Although we are not all called to sacrifice these goods, even those living in the world are called to place their love of God above the love of possessions, family, and self.

As we have seen, various religious communities have been officially instituted throughout history for those who are called to the religious life. There are communities for men and others for women. In both, members live a community life according to a particular rule. Prayer and contemplation ordered to a more perfect love of God and neighbor are the basic work of all religious communities. For some communities this is their principal work. These members of *contemplative* orders spend their days in prayer, by which they serve God and the entire Church. This is a great work that helps the world tremendously, since there are so many who forget God. The contemplatives usually live a *cloistered* life, separated completely from the world and working within their monasteries or convents to support themselves. The Benedictine and Cistercian communities, as well as some Carmelite communities, are examples of the contemplative religious life.

Other religious communities dedicate themselves to a more active service of God and neighbor by engaging in various works of mercy— both corporal and spiritual. These active orders may operate schools, hospitals, or orphanages. There is one community of sisters who both visit and pray for those in prison, helping them to reform their lives. This order has, in fact, many sisters who were once prisoners themselves. Mother Teresa's Missionaries of Charity are an active community who care for those who are dying and perform other active works. This active work, however, must always flow from and be an expression of the prayer life of these religious communities. Prayer, then, even in the active religious life is the basis for all their work.

Priesthood

There is a very special calling of Christ which is of great importance in the Church. It is not something one can simply choose, but something one is called to. It is the priesthood, the sacrament of Holy Orders. This call to exercise the priestly power of Christ and to be ''another Christ'' is a great honor but also a great and beautiful sacrifice. Those who have received Holy Orders share most perfectly in the redeeming work of Jesus Christ. They are the ministers of grace to the Church, as they administer the sacraments.

Some priests or clergy are members of a religious community. The clergy is made up of deacons, priests, and bishops. Most ordained ministers in the Church have been called to serve Christ as *diocesan clergy*. They are members of a particular diocese, often serving in parish work.

At their ordination the diocesan clergy promise obedience to their bishop, and bishops owe their obedience to the Pope. In the Latin rite the priests do not marry, taking a vow of *celibacy*. However, in the Latin rite permanent deacons may be married, and in some Eastern rites priests may be married. Those who are married do promise, however, not to marry again if their spouse dies. Diocesan clergy are not bound to take a vow of poverty. They may own things and usually receive a small salary for their personal expenses. They try to live a simple life in order to imitate Our Lord more closely and to be a witness for Christ to the world.

The Church needs many men and women to follow Christ, answering God's call to the religious life and the priesthood. We should pray to know if this is God's will for us. Even if this is not our vocation, we should pray that those who are called will joyfully respond, for:

The harvest is plentiful, but the laborers are few; pray therefore the Lord of the harvest to send out laborers into his harvest (Mt 9:37−38).

Words to Know:

evangelical counsels
celibacy   contemplative   clergy

Church Teaching

"This then is the primary purpose, this the central idea of Christian virginity: to aim only at the divine, to turn thereto the whole mind and soul; to want to please God in everything, to think of him continually, to consecrate body and soul to him."

(Holy Virginity, Pius XII, March 25, 1954)

Q. 63 *Is the priesthood a great dignity?*
The dignity of the priesthood is very great, because of its power over the real Body of Jesus Christ which is made present in the Holy Eucharist and because of its power over the Mystical Body of Jesus, the Church, which the priesthood rules and governs, with the sublime mission of leading men to holiness and to the life of the blessed.

Q. 64 *What purposes must he have in view who takes Holy Orders?*
He who takes Holy Orders must have as his purpose only the glory of God and the salvation of souls.

Q. 65 *Can a person enter into Holy Orders at his own will?*
No one may enter into Holy Orders at his own will but he must be called by God: in other words, he must have the *vocation* to Holy Orders, with the attitudes required by the sacred ministry.

"Father, you call all who believe in you to grow perfect in love by following in the footsteps of Christ your Son. May those whom you have chosen to serve you as religious provide by their way of life a convincing sign of your Kingdom for the Church and the whole world. We ask this through Our Lord Jesus Christ, your Son, who lives and reigns with you and the Holy Spirit, one God, for ever and ever. *Amen.*"

(Sacramentary, Mass for Religious Vocations)

CHAPTER 18

The Lay Apostolate

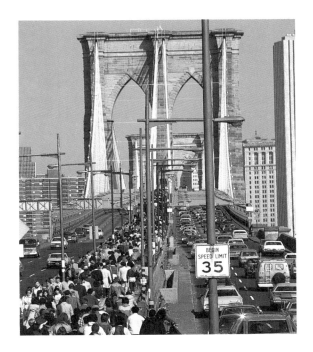

"From the fact of their union with Christ the head flows the laymen's right and duty to be apostles. Inserted as they are in the Mystical Body of Christ by baptism and strengthened by the power of the Holy Spirit in confirmation, it is by the Lord himself that they are assigned to the apostolate." (AA, 3).

While God calls some to serve him in the religious life or the priesthood, he calls most people to serve him in the world. Those members of the Church who are not ordained or do not belong to a religious community are called the *laity*.

The laity share the universal call to holiness with those in religious life. They, like priests, sisters, and brothers, must develop a strong spiritual life, uniting themselves with Christ through prayer, work, and the sacraments. This form of the spiritual life, however, will be different for each group because of their activities and obligations.

In addition to this universal call to holiness, members of the laity are also called to serve the Church in various capacities. This service begins within their individual parish communities. They may also serve the Church at the diocesan, national, or even international levels.

Finally, the laity, like the religious, are called to be witnesses of Christ and his Church. Both by their word and their example, laymen are called to bring Christ's gospel message to the world. Because their manner of life is the same as that of others in the world—raising families, working, and so on—they may at times be more effective witnesses of the gospel than are those in religious life.

Unlike priests and religious, who are called to live *separated from* the world, the layman must live *in* the world. He must "permeate society with the leaven of the gospel". The laity must be the "salt of the earth" (Mt 5:13), drawing the world to Christ. This means that they must try to bring Christian justice and charity into all the activities of human life—social, economic, industrial, political, cultural, and recreational activities.

All of these are temporal (worldly) goods, and it is the specific vocation of the layman to sanctify them. The grace of Christ does not take the place of nature but respects the natural order and perfects it.

The layman is especially called to use the three great goods that religious freely give up—wealth, sexuality, and independence. The laity are called to use their money and possessions for the good of the Church, of their families and of those in need. Most are also called to marry and raise a family, thus bringing new souls to Christ. Finally, they are called to use their freedom to make Christ present everywhere in the world.

Even though the layman's vocation is to live in the world, he must always keep in mind the warning of Our Lord that we live in the world but not be of the world. The laity must work to renew the temporal order, drawing all toward God. But at the same time, they must strive to keep themselves free from the corruptions of the world. St. Paul wrote, "Do not be conformed to this world" (Rom 12:2).

The lay apostolate encompasses both work and *leisure* (those activities that are not work

and are done for their own sake). The layman must sanctify himself as well as the world through these activities.

Each person is called to sanctify his ordinary labor, using it as a means of serving God. For you, as students, your principal "work" or duty right now is to study, learning basic skills and preparing yourself for future studies in high school. You must, then, use your studies and homework to praise God. This means

"Help me spread your fragrance everywhere. Flood my soul with your spirit and life. Penetrate and possess my whole being so utterly that all my life may be a witness, a radiance of yours. Shine through me and be so in me that every soul I come in contact with may be aware of your presence in me. Let them look up and see no longer me, but only you, Lord Jesus."

(Cardinal Newman)

Church Teaching

"Laymen ought to take on themselves as their distinctive task this renewal of the temporal order. Guided by the light of the gospel and the mind of the Church, prompted by Christian love, they should act in this domain in a different way and in their own specific manner. As citizens among citizens they must bring to their cooperation with others their own special competence and act on their own responsibility; everywhere and always they have to seek the justice of the Kingdom of God'' (AA, 7).

beginning now to do the best you can in your schoolwork, so that it may be a fitting offering to God. The same is true of any duties you may have at home—for example, doing the dishes, caring for the yard—or at a job. The layman is also called to sanctify his leisure—serving God through excellence in art, music, athletics, and the like.

The lay vocation embraces both the married and the unmarried life. Both are called to live chastity in different ways, according to their state. While most of the laity are called to the married state, there are some people who live the lay life as unmarried persons. These people continue to live in the world and have no intention of entering a religious community. While this calling may not be for many, those who are called to the single life in the world are given the graces they need to become holy through the sacrament of Confirmation. They also gain strength from the sacraments of Penance and the Eucharist.

The single state may be chosen by some people who desire to serve others in the world more fully than they could if they had a family. For example, it was common in our country in the last century for women teachers to remain unmarried, so that they could devote themselves more fully to educating others. Others may remain unmarried because obligations in justice or charity require it. For example, one might remain single in order to be able to care for aged parents or other relatives who need one's care.

Most lay people however, live the married life. This state is a great vocation, instituted and blessed by God at the Creation of the world. We will consider the married state in the next chapter.

Words to Know:

laity

CHAPTER 19

Marriage and the Family

"God created man in his own image and likeness: calling him to existence through love, *he called him at the same time* for love" *(FC, 11)*.

There are two main vocations to love: marriage and virginity or celibacy. The vocation to marriage is a vocation to a specific kind of human love (conjugal love), blessed by God and instituted by him at the creation of the world. In the first two chapters of Genesis we read about the creation of the world and the institution of married life.

In the above quote, the Pope refers to the words of Genesis 1:27 telling us that God made man and woman in his own image. This means that they are different from everything else in the world that God had created until then. They have an intellect and free will as God has. They are persons, a man and a woman, equal in dignity—"male and female he created them". God is love, and since they were made in his image they were made to love God and each other. The words of Genesis continue, "God blessed them". Thus they formed the first community of love, an image of the Trinity, which is the divine community of love.

Then God said to them, "Be fruitful and multiply, and fill the earth . . ." (Gen 1:28). This tells us that God meant this community of love, which is marriage, to bear fruit. He gave them a share in his act of creation. The fruit of marriage is children. This is its first purpose. God intended that through the loving union of man and woman in marriage, children be brought forth. They are its crowning glory.

In the second chapter of Genesis we read more about the vocation of marriage:

> The Lord God said, "It is not good that the man should be alone; I will make a helper fit for him" . . . and the rib which the Lord God had taken from the man he made into a woman and brought her to the man. Then the man said, "This at last is bone of my bones and flesh of my flesh. . . ." Therefore a man leaves his father and mother and cleaves to his wife, and they become one flesh (Gen 2:18, 22–24).

Here God reveals to us that marriage, which by its nature is a union of love, has as a second purpose *mutual love* and *support* of the husband and wife. The man and woman united in marriage are to support one another in life. They are to help one another in their tasks on earth—primarily raising their children. Through marriage they become *one* and are no longer simply individuals. They are called to sacrifice some of their individual freedom for the sake of a greater good—the new family they have formed.

We also learn from the above quote that the man and woman shall become one flesh—that is, the union in marriage is one of body as well as of soul. There is a total giving, under God, of the whole person to the other. There can be no total conjugal self-giving apart from marriage. Total self-giving means giving of oneself, until death, exclusively to one person. You enter freely and consciously into marriage. You make a public promise in front of witnesses which, once made, you are no longer free to take back. You even give up the right to decide otherwise in the future. Total giving of self also means accepting all the consequences, which includes openness to the gift of life.

Since bodily union is an expression of the total self-giving of two persons, it is a lie if it takes place between two unmarried persons. If your body expresses, ''I am yours for ever'', but your mind knows that is not true, then you are lying. That is why sex outside of marriage is a lie. It is also, of course, fornication or adultery.

The Sacrament of Marriage

The married state has been blessed by Our Lord, as well. At the beginning of his public life, Our Lord attended a wedding feast where he worked his first miracle (Jn 2:1−11). By his presence at this wedding, Christ blessed the vocation of marriage. He also raised marriage above the natural level to the dignity of a sacrament. Thus, the baptized man and woman who unite themselves in marriage receive from Christ the graces that they need to live this life. These are special graces to help them overcome obstacles, bear their crosses, and become better spouses and parents.

For the Christian the natural ends, or purposes, of marriage are raised to a supernatural level. The bearing and raising of children are not simply for life here on earth. Christian parents raise children that they may eventually be united for ever with God in Heaven. Similarly, the Christian husband and wife not only support one another in mutual love but, even more importantly, must help one another to know, love, and serve God so that they may reach Heaven. This is called the *mutual sanctification* of the spouses.

Christ also emphasized the *indissoluble* nature of marriage. He taught us that the union of husband and wife is a lifelong union, which ends only with death. On one occasion, when Our Lord was questioned by the Pharisees about divorce, he quoted the passage from the second chapter of Genesis and then said:

What therefore God has joined together, let no man put asunder. . . . I say to you,

107

whoever divorces his wife . . . and marries another, commits adultery; and he who marries a divorced woman commits adultery (Mt 19:6, 9).

Thus did Our Lord make clear that marriage must be a permanent state on earth. He himself taught this on his authority as Son of God, for even in the Gospels we see that his contemporaries accepted divorce. Because the indissolubility of marriage is often rejected in today's world as well, the Christian must be an example and witness to the world.

The New Testament also teaches us about the supernatural element of marriage. In his letter to the Christian community in Ephesus, St. Paul reminds us of the mutual obligation of husbands and wives to love one another: "Husbands, love your wives, as Christ loved the Church . . . and let the wife see that she respects her husband" (Eph 5:25, 33). Thus, we are to love one another with Christ himself as our model.

The Family

As we have seen, husband and wife unite in marriage to form a new community—the family. The family is the basic unit of society. It is in the family that new human beings are brought into the world. It is here that we first learn how to live in society. And it is in the family that children are first taught and prepared for their place in the Church and in society. There are then obligations for both parents and children in the family.

In addition to helping one another to serve God and neighbor and thus reach Heaven, the state of marriage places other obligations and responsibilities on the husband and wife in their roles as parents. The first obligation is that they must be open to the gift of life. This

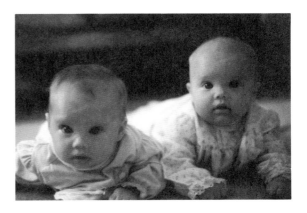

means that they must accept children as coming from God and destined for God. While it is true that not all marriages will be blessed with children, this openness to children must always be present. In such childless marriages the couples can glorify God through their union of love and their mutual sanctification. They are called to be spiritually fruitful through works of mercy such as, for instance, adoption or foster care of children.

The second obligation of parents is to care for those children whom God has given them. The basic needs of life must be met first. Satisfying physical needs, however, is not sufficient for preparing children for the world or for eternal life.

The third obligation of parents is to educate and form their children so that they will be able to lead good and useful lives on earth and, finally, to attain salvation in Heaven. Naturally, parents must see to the basic instruction of their children—reading, mathematics, and the like. More importantly, parents are responsible for their moral and religious education. They must care for the spiritual needs of their children —not simply their physical needs. One of the first duties of Christian parents, for example, is to have their children baptized.

Since moral, religious, and intellectual education begin very early in life, parents are the first teachers of their children, by both word and example. They are also the *primary* educators of their children. This means that the obligation for educating their children belongs first to the parents. Even though most parents eventually delegate their role of educator to the school, they should not abandon their role as the primary educators. Parents must continue to teach their children and help to form their moral characters.

Filial Piety

Children also have obligations and duties within the family, and must develop the virtue known as *filial piety*. This is the virtue of giving honor and respect to our parents, who are immediately responsible for our existence and well-being. Like the virtue of religion, filial piety is a part of justice and is an acknowledgement of the debt that we owe to our parents.

Filial piety requires us to obey our parents since they have been given authority from God to raise us. In this we can model ourselves on Jesus, who was obedient to Mary and Joseph. "And he went down with them and came to Nazareth and was obedient to them" (Lk 2:51). This obligation is proper to us until we reach adulthood and are responsible for our own lives.

Filial piety, however, does not end with our maturity. We are still obliged to honor and respect our parents. We must recognize the great work they have undertaken with God and should show them esteem and gratitude. That is what the Fourth Commandment is all about.

Finally, filial piety requires us to care for our parents in their old age or infirmity. The Word of God in the book of Sirach reminds us of this duty: "O son, help your father in his old age, and do not grieve him as long as he lives" (Sir 3:12).

Behold how good and pleasant it is when brothers dwell in unity (Ps 133:1).

Children also have the duty within the family to love and respect their brothers and sisters. This charity should be offered to everyone, but since we share a more intimate bond with the members of our family, it is even more important there. Often this is difficult to achieve, but we must each work to make our homes centers of Christian charity and unity.

Finally, children also have an obligation to respect the authority belonging to those who teach them. Since parents may delegate some of their authority to the school, just as they respect, honor, and obey their parents, children must respect, honor, and obey those who teach them. We recognize this special role of the school as taking the place of our parents temporarily when we call the school our *alma mater*, which means "loving or nourishing mother". Truly we are nourished by the school as we are nourished by our parents.

In addition to this, as children grow older, they must take upon themselves more and more responsibility for their education. This is particularly important in our religious education. Often people study their faith during their youth, are confirmed, and then do not pay any further attention to their religious development. Our knowledge of our faith does not end with our Confirmation. Rather, we must, as adults in the Church, take charge of our religious development and continue to grow in the knowledge and love of God.

The married state, through family life, prepares us for our place in society. In the next chapter we will examine the role of the Christian in the state and the world.

Words to Know:

filial piety

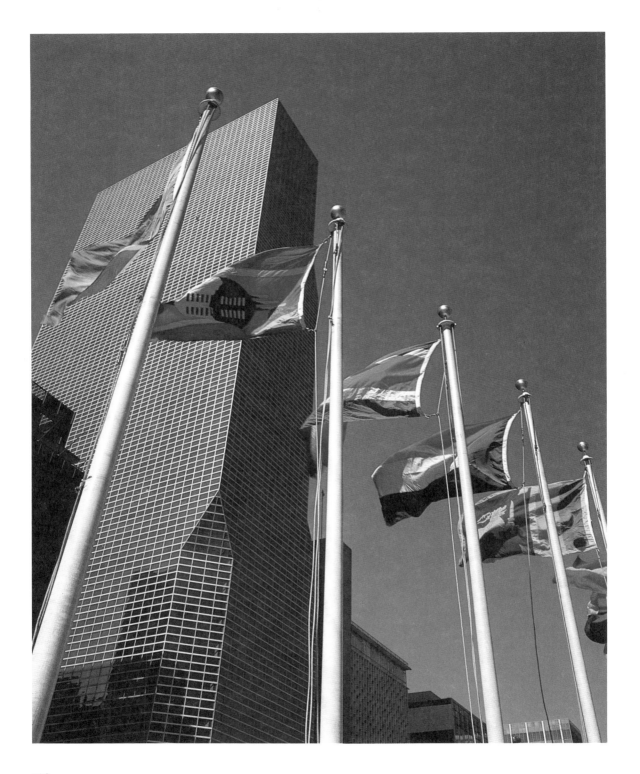

CHAPTER 20

The Christian in the World

"By me kings reign, and rulers decree what is just; by me princes rule, and nobles govern the earth" (Prov 8:15−16).

Just as men and women naturally come together to form families, human beings also join together to form larger societies. Not only are we members of a family, but we are citizens of a city or town, state, and a nation. Just as our parents have legitimate authority over us in the family, so do the officials of the civil government. St. Paul reminds us that their authority, like that of our parents, comes from God:

> Let every person be subject to the governing authorities. For there is no authority except from God. . . . Therefore he who resists the authorities resists what God has appointed. . . (Rom 13:1−2).

The purpose of civil society is to promote and ensure the *common good* of its members. The common good is the welfare of the whole community, not just an individual. In order to promote the common good of the whole community the state has the authority to make just (fair) laws and regulations to govern its citizens. And citizens have an obligation to obey and respect these laws. Our Lord taught us the importance of recognizing civil authority when he was asked about the lawfulness of paying tribute to Caesar, "Render to Caesar the things that are Caesar's, and to God the things that are God's" (Lk 20:25). It is important to remember that in this passage Our Lord gives two commands. As Christians we must first of all obey the laws of God. Then, as citizens, we must obey the laws of society.

God's Laws Come First

While the civil government—sometimes called "the state"—has legitimate authority, it does not have the right to demand something which violates God's law. For example, no government has the right to command willful murder, since this is a violation of God's law. When such laws are made, citizens are not bound to obey them. In fact, in some sense they are not really laws. In such a situation we should think of the words of St. Peter to the Sanhedrin, "We must obey God rather than men" (Acts 5:29).

To illustrate this point—that God's law is above the law of the state—we can look at the life of St. Thomas More. Thomas More was a great lawyer and statesman in England at the beginning of the sixteenth century. He was a layman who dedicated himself to serving his country and his king. He rose to prominence during the reign of his friend King Henry VIII and was eventually appointed Chancellor of England, second in power to the king.

In order to divorce his wife, King Henry declared himself to be the supreme head of the Church in England. All of his subjects were then required to take an oath acknowledging this and declaring their primary allegiance to the king. Thomas More knew that he could not take this oath, for that would mean denying God's law.

On July 6, 1535, Thomas More was beheaded —by order of the king and his court—for refusing to sign the oath. Before he died, he reminded us that God's law is supreme: "I die the king's good servant, but God's first."

Civil Laws

Although we are not bound to obey such laws, we are bound to obey all laws which conform to God's laws. For example, we must obey laws regarding the property rights of others. In addition to obeying just laws, there are several other duties which we have as citizens.

As citizens we must develop the virtue of *patriotism*, which is love of one's country. It is natural and good for us to love our native land. Patriotism is not merely the emotional reaction we may have when we sing our national anthem or see our nation's flag. This emotional reaction may be the beginning. However, patriotism is actually a deep love for our country which prompts us to dedicate ourselves to promoting those things which are good for our country and its citizens.

At the same time, we must avoid that excessive love of country which can result in the error of excessive *nationalism*. This can result from a love which is blind to the defects of one's nation. One must also avoid the opposite error which is a lack of love for one's country which can lead one to despise and turn against one's own country. The actual betrayal of one's country is known as *treason*.

The Christian citizen must use his influence to help make his nation just. This is an area in which the laity are especially called to bring Christ to the world. We must work to promote just and moral laws, in keeping with God's law. When there are unjust laws, we must work to change them. We must work to change harmful attitudes such as racism and lack of respect for human beings, including the unborn and the poor, by conforming our own attitudes to justice, truth, and love. In a democratic nation, the Christian, then, has a particular duty to take part in the government of his country—voting for good leaders or perhaps even running for office himself.

Duties of Citizens

There are also other duties which we have as citizens. We must support the government through the payment of taxes and we should, if necessary, be willing to defend our country against unjust aggression. Finally, as Christians we have a particular obligation to pray for our leaders and our country.

Besides being citizens of our nation, we are

"You must obey all the governing authorities. Since all government comes from God, the civil authorities were appointed by God. . . . The state is there to serve God for your benefit."

(Rom 13:1—4)

also members of the larger society of the world. We cannot isolate ourselves in our own nation, but we must be concerned about all peoples. As Christians we have a responsibility to serve others—particularly those whose rights and human needs are not recognized. We must work for peace and justice in the world, practicing the corporal works of mercy wherever we can.

The Christian View of Creatures

In the first chapter of Genesis we read of the creation of the world. Out of nothing God brought into existence all the creatures of our world. First he created many inanimate objects —the sun, the moon, the mountains, and the seas. Then he made the various plants and the many animals—birds, fish, insects, and the beasts of the earth. Finally, as the pinnacle of his creation on earth, God created man and woman and said to them:

Fill the earth and subdue it; and have dominion over the fish of the sea and over the birds of the air and over every living thing that moves upon the earth (Gen 1:28).

When God created the world he gave human beings *dominion* over his creation. This means that God made the earth and all of the creatures on it—animals, plants, mountains, rivers, etc. —for us. They were made, first of all, to glorify God and to remind us of him and lead us to himself—as does, for example, a magnificent sunset. But these things were also made to give us joy.

Because we are the highest creatures on earth, we have been entrusted with a great responsibility to exercise *stewardship* over creation. This means that we must take care of creation and use wisely the many gifts God has given us. We must not waste or abuse any of God's creation. Man depends on air, water, forests, plants, and animals for his life, food, and clothing. Stewardship does not mean that we cannot kill animals for these purposes, but we must use them for our needs, not wastefully. Nor should we cause animals any unnecessary suffering but treat them kindly.

St. Francis of Assisi can be an example for us of the care we should have for all God's creatures. Francis loved not only the poor of this world but all of God's creatures as well— animals and all of nature. He saw all of creation as traces and reflections of God. His tenderness for and his gentle sway over animals were often noted by his companions. He spoke of animals and indeed, all creatures, as his ''brothers'' and ''sisters''. His beautiful ''Canticle of the Sun'' illustrates this reverence for God's work.

Words to Know:

common good   stewardship

patriotism

Q. 63 *Why are we obliged to obey superiors in authority?*
We are obliged to obey superiors in authority because ''there is no authority except from God; . . . as a consequence, the man who opposes authority rebels against the ordinance of God'' (Rom 13:1−2).

Canticle of the Sun

Oh, Most High, Almighty, Good Lord God, to thee belong praise, glory, honor and all blessing.

Praised be my Lord God, with all his creatures, and especially our brother the Sun, who brings us the day and who brings us the light: fair is he, and he shines with a very great splendor.

O Lord, he signifies thee to us!

Praised be my Lord for our sister the Moon, and for the stars, the which he has set clear and lovely in the heaven.

Praised be my Lord for our brother the wind, and for air and clouds, calms and all weather, by which thou upholdest life and all creatures.

Praised be my Lord for our sister water, who is very serviceable to us, and humble and precious and clean.

Praised be my Lord for our brother fire, through whom thou givest us light in the darkness; and he is bright and pleasant and very mighty and strong.

Praised be my Lord for our mother the earth, the which doth sustain us and keep us, and bringeth forth divers fruits and flowers of many colors, and grass.

Praised be my Lord for all those who pardon one another for love's sake, and who endure weakness and tribulation: blessed are they who peacefully shall endure, for thou, O Most High, wilt give them a crown.

Praised be my Lord for our sister, the death of the body, from which no man escapeth. Woe to him who dieth in mortal sin. Blessed are those who die in thy most holy will, for the second death shall have no power to do them harm.

Praise ye and bless the Lord, and give thanks to him and serve him with great humility.

CHAPTER 21

Law and Conscience

"The law is holy, and the commandment is holy and just and good" (Rom 7:12).

When we look at the world we see that everything operates according to a certain plan or order. For example, rivers flow toward the sea, birds build nests each spring for their young, and when we drop a stone it falls to the ground. As Creator of the world, God has provided for all of his creatures. In his *providence* he governs all things, directing and ordering each to its proper end or purpose. This is the *eternal law* of God which encompasses all creatures on earth.

The chart on the next page shows that from God, the Eternal Law, all laws come. Let us examine each of these sorts of law.

Physical Laws

God's eternal law is first divided into *physical laws* and *moral laws*. *Physical laws*, also called *laws of nature*, are those which govern the nature and operation of all material things and natural forces. The law of gravity or other laws of physics and chemistry are examples of physical laws. The instincts of animals, which cause them to act in particular ways, are also physical laws. The laws which govern the physical world can neither be disobeyed nor repealed.

The laws which direct our will toward the good are called *moral laws*. Since human beings have free wills, the laws which guide our actions can be broken. We are always free to choose good or evil. Such laws help us to direct our wills toward their proper purpose— perfection on earth and, finally, happiness in Heaven.

Blessed are those whose way is blameless, who walk in the law of the Lord! . . . who also do no wrong, but walk in his ways! (Ps 119:1, 3).

The entire moral law comes to us from God. Part of it comes directly from him, but another part of it comes indirectly from him through a human lawgiver. The first part, *divine law*, is divided into two sorts—*natural law* and *revealed law*.

Divine Law

Natural Law

The *natural law* is the basic moral law which God has placed in human nature and which we discover through reason. This law is written in the hearts of men, and its most basic principle is "Do good and avoid evil." However, because of original sin, which has clouded our intellects, we do not always recognize

LAW
God—the Eternal Law

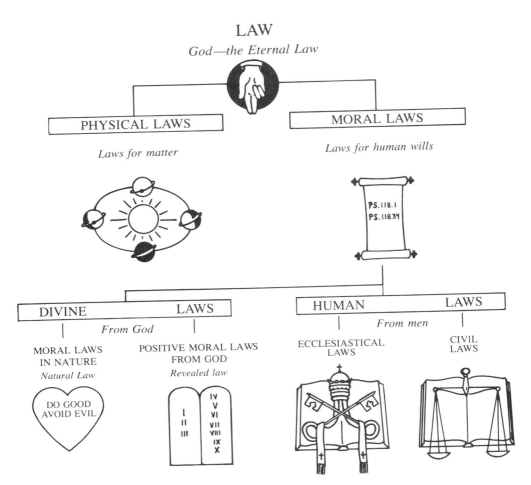

PHYSICAL LAWS

Laws for matter

MORAL LAWS

Laws for human wills

PS.118.1
PS.118.34

DIVINE   **LAWS**

From God

HUMAN   **LAWS**

From men

MORAL LAWS
IN NATURE
Natural Law

DO GOOD
AVOID EVIL

POSITIVE MORAL LAWS
FROM GOD
Revealed law

I II III IV V VI VII VIII IX X

ECCLESIASTICAL
LAWS

CIVIL
LAWS

what is good and what is evil. Most people, even pagans, can easily see that certain things, like murder, stealing, or lying are wrong. However, it is not so easy to see that at times it can be wrong to say something which is actually true. For example, spreading facts that would deliberately harm or embarrass another person might be seriously wrong.

Revealed Law

Because human beings often find it difficult to know what is right and wrong on their own, God has also revealed certain commandments to us. This is what we call *positive* or *revealed law*. These are the commandments which are contained in the Old Law given through Moses at Mount Sinai and the New Law given by Our Lord when he was on earth. The Old Law was given by God in the Old Testament—for example, the Ten Commandments. This law was the first stage of God's revelation and by itself is incomplete. This law was perfected in the New Testament. Our Lord said: "Think not that I have come to abolish the law and the prophets; I have come not to abolish them but to fulfill them" (Mt 5:17). Our Lord tells us to keep his law out of love rather than out of fear (Jn 14:15). While the Ten Commandments are examples of revealed laws given in the Old Testament, the forbidding of divorce by Jesus (Mt 19:1−9) is an example of a revealed law from the New Testament. It is important to recall that the Church's magisterium is the authentic interpreter of divine law, that is, of both the natural law and positive revealed law.

Many of the revealed precepts repeat and confirm points in the natural law which men might discover on their own. God repeats these —for example, ''Thou shalt not kill'', ''Thou shalt not steal''—because of their importance. Other precepts require God's revelation if we are to know them. Thus, for example, God tells us that we are to worship him on a particular day each week.

Human Laws

Many moral laws are made by humans themselves and are called *human laws*. Human laws are divided into *civil laws* and *ecclesiastical* (Church) *laws*. Civil laws are those made by the civil authorities. Laws regarding the payment of taxes or traffic laws are examples.

Ecclesiastical laws are those made by the Church. There are many of these, and they are contained in the book of Canon Law. However, seven of them are particularly important for all Catholics and we should know them. They are:

1. To keep holy the day of the Lord's Resurrection: to worship God by participating in Mass every Sunday and Holy Day of Obligation (see the list in Chapter 8): to avoid those activities that would hinder renewal of soul and body, e.g., needless work and business activities, unnecessary shopping, etc.

2. To lead a sacramental life: to receive Holy Communion frequently and the sacrament of Penance regularly:
—minimally, to confess grave sins in the sacrament of Penance at least once a year (annual confession is obligatory only if serious sin is involved).
—minimally, to receive Holy Communion at least once a year, between the First Sunday of Lent and Trinity Sunday.

3. To study Catholic teaching in preparation for the sacrament of Confirmation, to be confirmed, and then to continue to study and advance the cause of Christ.

4. To observe the marriage laws of the Church: to give religious training (by example and word) to one's children; to use parish schools and religious education programs.

5. To strengthen and support the Church: one's own parish community and parish priests; the worldwide Church and the Holy Father.

Church Teaching

''. . . In forming their consciences the faithful must pay careful attention to the sacred and certain teaching of the Church. For the Catholic Church is, by the will of Christ, the teacher of truth. It is her duty to proclaim and teach with authority the truth which is Christ and, at the same time, to declare and confirm by her authority the principles of the moral order which spring from human nature itself'' (DH, 14).

6. To do penance, including abstaining from meat and fasting from food on the appointed days:
—abstaining on Ash Wednesday and all the Fridays of Lent;
—fasting on Ash Wednesday and Good Friday.

7. To join in the missionary spirit and apostolate of the Church.

Sometimes the government and the Church repeat and reaffirm divine laws. For example, a state may have laws against murder or stealing, and the Church also teaches us that these actions are wrong. Such laws, though repeated by men, are *not* human laws. They are *divine laws*. It is important to understand this because these laws cannot be changed by men.

We must also realize that there is a hierarchy among laws; for example, God's laws are higher than man's. Thus if a law of man is in conflict with or contradicts a law of God, we must follow God's law. This was what Thomas More did, as we saw in the last chapter.

When we speak of laws we speak of both the *spirit* and the *letter* of the law. The spirit is the understanding behind the law and the letter is the actual words of the law. In following these laws we must follow both the spirit and the letter.

There is a clear difference between the law and legalism. Christ said, "It is easier for Heaven and earth to pass away than for one dot of the law to become void" (Lk 16:17). On the other hand, he severely rebuked the Pharisees for their legalism. They had forgotten all about the spirit behind the law, while holding fast to the letter. Thus they made the law void. For instance, there was a tradition among them that if you said to your parents that you were dedicating your goods to God, then you were no longer obliged to help and honor them.

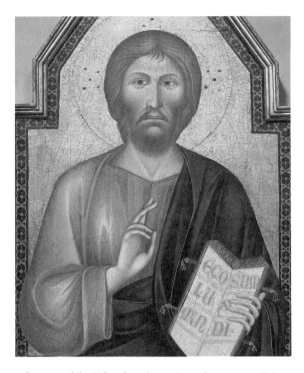

Jesus said, "So for the sake of your tradition you have made void the Word of God. You hypocrites! Well did Isaiah prophesy of you when he said, 'This people honors me with their lips, but their heart is far from me' " (Mt 15:7−9). Time and again Christ showed that the law of charity is supreme. It does not void the law but fulfills it. St. Paul reminds us: "Above all these things have love" (Col 3:14).

Conscience

Besides the external guide of the moral law, God has also given us an internal guide to help us determine which actions are good and which are bad. This is known as our *conscience*. Many of us may think of our conscience as a 'little voice'—like Jimminy Cricket—which tells us what to do or scolds us when we do wrong. This is a false understanding of conscience.

Conscience is a specific action of our reason, or intellect, by which we judge the rightness or wrongness of a particular action. It is not a feeling or emotion. Conscience is the application of certain principles—found in the moral law—to a specific, concrete moral situation.

In order to be of any use to us, our conscience must be correctly *formed* or taught. We are obliged to follow our conscience, but we are also obliged to make sure that our conscience is properly formed.

When our conscience is correctly formed and the judgments which we make are correct, we have a *true* conscience. If our judgments are incorrect we have a *false* conscience. A false conscience is lax if it fails to see sin where sin actually exists. For example, our conscience is lax if we do not think deliberately missing Mass on Sunday is a serious sin. A false conscience is scrupulous if it magnifies the gravity of sin or finds sin where there really is none. For example, our conscience is scrupulous if we think that missing Sunday Mass when we are very ill is a sin. Such false consciences have not been correctly formed.

To form our conscience we must look to the Church, which speaks the Word of God to us today, and we must listen to her voice. At the same time we should try to understand these laws of God so that we may be better able to follow them.

Words to Know:

eternal law   natural law
civil law   ecclesiastical law
moral law   divine law
conscience

Church Teaching

"It is through his conscience that man sees and recognizes the demands of the divine law. He is bound to follow this conscience faithfully in all his activity so that he may come to God, who is his last end. Therefore he must not be forced to act contrary to his conscience. Nor must he be prevented from acting according to his conscience, especially in religious matters" (DH, 3).

CHAPTER 22

The Church and The Social Order

"Go therefore and make disciples of all nations, baptizing them in the name of the Father and of the Son and of the Holy Spirit, teaching them to observe all that I have commanded you. . ." (Mt 28:19–20).

Immediately before the Ascension, Our Lord stood on the mountain in Galilee and said these words to his apostles. This final command tells us of the duty to spread the gospel to every man. But Our Lord meant more than baptizing individuals. He told the apostles to baptize all nations. This means to infuse society with the message of the gospel—to *form Christian nations*.

The Church's duty then extends beyond drawing individuals to Christ. The Church must also help to shape society so that the public morality will be Christian. In this way the Church "baptizes" the social order, so that all things may be renewed in Christ.

In Scripture we find mentioned four sins which "cry to Heaven for vengeance". They are sodomy (perverse sexual behavior), willful murder, oppression of the poor, and defrauding the laborer of his just wage. These sins do not "cry to Heaven" because they are the most serious sins. Idolatry and blasphemy, for ex-

ample, are even worse. These four sins, however, are all injustices which undermine the fundamental order of society—particularly the family, the basic unit of society. Because of their effect on society, the Church, over the centuries, has often addressed these matters in her social teachings.

Much of the Church's social teaching may be found in the *encyclicals* of the popes. These letters addressed to all the bishops and the entire Church are also a means of instructing the world and bringing the gospel to all nations. As we consider the last three of the sins which cry out to Heaven, we will mention some of these encyclicals. Because they are addressed to the entire Church, they were written originally in the universal language of the Church—Latin. Below, the Latin title of each encyclical is given with the English title in parentheses.

Protection of Human Life

"Cain rose up against his brother Abel, and killed him. Then the Lord said to Cain, 'Where is Abel your brother? . . . What have you done? The voice of your brother's blood is crying to me from the ground' " (Gen 4:8–10).

Murder was the first sin committed after the Fall. God, in speaking to Cain, tells us of the grave injustice which has been done. Yet, we know that not all killing is necessarily wrong. If Abel had killed Cain in self-defense this would not have been murder. Murder is the unjust taking of innocent life, which is what Cain did. This is also what is meant by the Fifth Commandment "Thou shalt not kill."

In modern times one of the most serious forms of willful murder is the killing of unborn children in the wombs of their mothers—*abortion*. This is the destruction of the most innocent and helpless human life. It destroys the future of our families and society. Abortion is certainly a sin which cries out to Heaven.

Through her teachings the Church has always tried to protect human life from such injustices. During the twentieth century, when the practice of abortion has spread to many nations— including our own—the popes have frequently addressed the world on this matter. They have proclaimed the sacredness of human life from conception until natural death and the importance of the family, where new life begins and is nurtured. Two important social encyclicals which speak on these matters are *Casti Connubii* (Christian Marriage) by Pope Pius XI and *Humanae Vitae* (Of Human Life) by Pope Paul VI.

War and Peace

The Church has always taught that just as it is licit for a person to defend himself or his family or defenseless persons against attack, so it is licit for nations to defend themselves or help others defend themselves against unjust aggression. This is what is known as a just war. Of course, first, other avenues for stopping the attack must be considered and used, if possible and effective. Also, the response to an attack must not be out of proportion. The moral principle used is: "preserving the moderation of blameless defense".

The Second Vatican Council taught:

> Every act of war directed to the indiscriminate destruction of whole cities or vast areas with their inhabitants is a crime against God and man, which merits firm and unequivocal condemnation (GS, 80).

As far as nuclear deterrence is concerned Pope John Paul II stated that

> under present conditions, deterrence based on equilibrium—certainly not as an end in itself, but as a stage on the way to progressive disarmament—can still be judged to be morally acceptable. However, to insure peace it is indispensable not to be content with a minimum which is always fraught with a real danger of explosion (Message to the United Nations, June 1982).

Several national bishops' conferences have issued Pastoral Letters on the question of war and peace, for instance, the U.S. bishops and the French bishops. They agree on the basic principles, but also agree that the practical application may differ because prudential judgments are involved.

Social Justice

"You shall not wrong a stranger or oppress him . . . you shall not afflict any widow or orphan. If you do afflict them, and they cry out to me, I will surely hear their cry. . . (Ex 22:21—23).

"Behold the wages of the laborers who mowed your fields, which you kept back by fraud, cry out, and . . . have reached the ears of the Lord . . ." (James 5:4).

Oppressing the poor, the widowed, the orphaned, etc., and defrauding the laborer of his wage are also sins which directly harm society. These two evils are the basis of the Church's teaching on economic and civic matters. The Church reminds all people and nations of their obligations in justice to care for the unfortunate among us. Thus, the Church teaches us of the evils of economic systems that exploit the poor.

The Church also teaches us of the importance of paying the laborer a fair wage. Families cannot survive unless the heads of households are paid enough to provide for their basic needs—food, clothing, and shelter.

These teachings on economic issues have been particularly emphasized during the last one hundred years. The popes have written a number of important encyclicals on these topics. The first, in 1891, which is the basis for all those which followed, was *Rerum Novarum* (The Condition of Labor) by Pope Leo XIII. A more recent one, called *Laborem Exercens* (The Dignity of Labor), was written by Pope John Paul II.

In our concern for the promotion of the dignity of man, we must note that not every movement, ideology, or form of government which claims to benefit man or the poor does so. Certain movements in the twentieth century have been condemned by the Church. Communism, while claiming to be for the oppressed classes in society, actually exploits them and suppresses basic human rights. National Socialism (Nazism) claimed the superiority of one race, and the Nazis brutally enslaved and persecuted others, even committing mass genocide. Any form of racism is condemned by the Church, since we are all created in God's image and Christ died for each one of us. Consequently, the Church has taught about the evils of these systems. Pope Pius XI wrote two encyclicals on these matters—*Mit Brennender Sorge* (Against the Nationalist State) and *Divini Redemptoris* (On Atheistic Communism).

These social teachings remind us of our Christian call to live in the world without adopting the ways of the world. At various times in history, people have ignored the Church's guidance and lived in ways contrary to the gospel. Our task is to reshape the values of society, if we can. At all times, even if the world is against us, we must listen to and follow the Church.

Words to Know:

just war   abortion

Church Teaching

"But at all times and in all places the Church should have true freedom to preach the faith, to proclaim its teaching about society, to carry out its task among men without hindrance, and to pass moral judgments even in matters relating to politics, whenever the fundamental rights of man or the salvation of souls requires it" (GS, 76).

Titus Brandsma

On July 26, 1942, at Dachau (one of the Nazi concentration camps in Germany), a Carmelite priest from the Netherlands was killed. Titus Brandsma was sixty-one years old, and he had spent the past thirty-seven years as a priest. How did he end up as a Nazi prisoner?

When Titus joined a Carmelite monastery in Holland in 1898, he began a lifetime of prayer and study. He initiated several different literary projects, writing on religious topics for various newspapers and magazines and encouraging others in his order to do the same. He was well prepared for such work by his education in philosophy and theology, and he used his writing to teach others.

Eventually he was appointed to the faculty of the Catholic University in the Netherlands. While he taught there he continued his other writing projects as well.

Some years later he was appointed by the bishops to be the spiritual advisor to the many lay staff members of the country's Catholic newspapers. It was this position that brought him to the attention of the Nazi leaders.

The Nazis invaded the Netherlands in 1940 and began immediately to repress the freedom of the Dutch peoples. Those who objected were immediately marked as traitors. Catholics were among those who resisted, and they began to suffer for this.

All newspapers—including Catholic papers—were ordered to print the press releases and advertisements which came from the Nazi government. Titus, as spiritual advisor to the Catholic journalists, traveled from city to city explaining to them that they must resist this pressure. Because of this, finally he was arrested.

When he was asked why he disobeyed the regulations, he said, ''As a Catholic, I could have done nothing differently. We must object to anything or any philosophy that is not in line with Catholic doctrine.'' Father Titus Brandsma understood the role of the Christian in the world, and he was not afraid to suffer for it.

PART THREE

The Means to Fulfill Our Call to Holiness

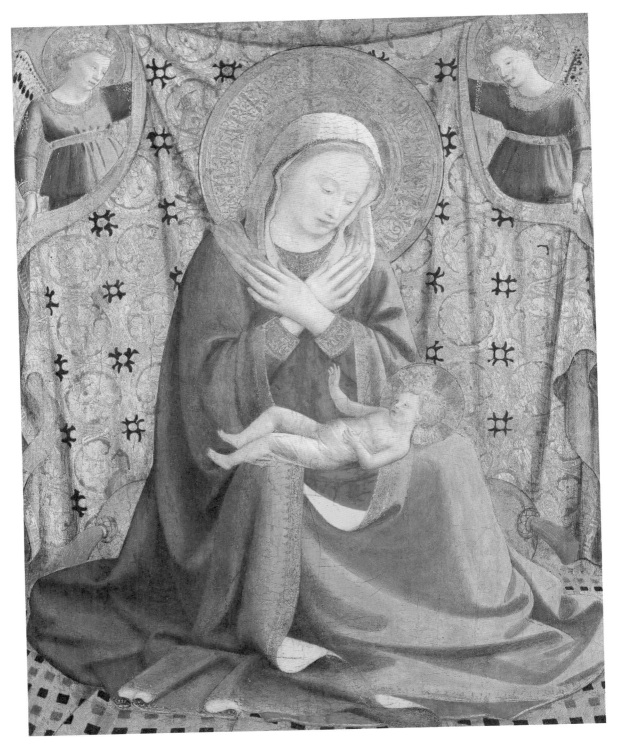

CHAPTER 23

Prayer

"Pray at all times in the Spirit, with all prayer and supplication" (Eph 6:13).

As Christians we are called to sanctify our lives and unite ourselves with Christ. The two principal means for accomplishing this are *prayer* and the *sacraments*.

Prayer is the lifting up of our minds and hearts to God. Just as the spoken word is our way of communicating with friends, so prayer is our way of conversing with God. Every thought of God—short or long—can be a prayer. For example, we might acknowledge the sovereignty of God or express gratitude to him for blessings he has given us. Or we might simply express our love for him. All of these are prayers.

Prayer is essential to our spiritual lives, as we can see from the Gospels. During his public life Our Lord often prayed. For example, he prayed in the desert before beginning his public ministry, he prayed on the mountain before he was transfigured, and he prayed in the Garden of Gethsemane on the night before he died. By these actions he taught us the importance of prayer.

But Jesus did not only teach us by example; he frequently spoke to the apostles about the necessity of prayer. At one point he told the apostles that they ". . . ought to pray always and not lose heart" (Lk 18:1). Here he told us

that we need to pray—even when it is difficult. There are times, for example, when various thoughts may distract us from our prayer. Such distractions may discourage us and tempt us to quit, but Jesus tells us that we should continue. Although these distractions are not always our fault, we should still work to draw our thoughts back to God as a sign of our love for him.

How should we pray? First, before we pray we should *prepare* ourselves to turn our thoughts to God. We should try to dismiss all other thoughts from our minds and direct our attention to God. Sometimes visible reminders—such as statues or paintings—will help us to concentrate on God. Next, we should pray with *humility*, like the tax collector in one of the parables told by Jesus (Lk 18:9−14). In addition, we should have *faith* and *confidence* that God will hear our prayer. As Our Lord said to his disciples at the Last Supper:

> Truly, truly, I say to you, if you ask anything of the Father, he will give it to you in my name (Jn 16:23).

Fourth, we should pray with *resignation* to the will of God, as Our Lord did on the eve of his death. That means that we accept how he answers our prayers. Finally, we should pray with *perseverance*. This means that we should keep on praying even if it seems as if God has

> I beseech you, O Lord, that the fiery and honey-sweet strength of your love may free my soul from all that is under Heaven, that I may die out of love for you, who deigned to die out of love for me. *Amen*.
>
> Prayer of St. Francis

not heard our prayer. To illustrate this point, Our Lord told the following parable:

> Which of you who has a friend will go to him at midnight and say to him, "Friend, lend me three loaves; for a friend of mine has arrived on a journey, and I have nothing to set before him"; and he will answer from within, "Do not bother me; the door is now shut, and my children are with me in bed; I cannot get up and give you anything"? I tell you, though he will not get up and give him anything because he is his friend, yet because of his importunity [persistence] he will rise and give him whatever he needs (Lk 11:5—8).

There are two forms of prayer—*mental* and *vocal*. Mental prayer is that which is said interiorly. Such prayer unites our hearts with God while we meditate on his holy truths. It usually begins with meditation—for example, on a passage from Scripture or one of the mysteries of our faith—which stirs our hearts to love God and unite ourselves with him. A good opportunity to pray in this manner is after we receive Our Lord in Holy Communion.

Vocal prayer is said by spoken words—alone or with others. However, the words alone are not prayer, as the prophet Isaiah reminded the people of the Old Testament:

> This people draw near with their mouth and honor me with their lips, while their hearts are far from me (Is 29:13).

We must join our hearts and minds to the words that we speak.

Vocal prayer may be *formal* or *informal*. Formal prayers are those that follow a set pattern or formula. These prayers use words composed by someone else—for example, Our Lord, the angel Gabriel, or one of the saints. The Our Father, the Hail Mary, the Memorare, and the Act of Contrition are all examples of formal prayers. The Psalms of the Old Testament, written by David and inspired by God, are also formal prayers. There are many times when such prayers help us to communicate our thoughts to God. They show us how we ought to pray. They lift our minds and hearts and fill us with heavenly desires and right attitudes. These prayers also unite us with other members of the Body of Christ, who pray the same prayers.

At other times it is good to use our own words to pray. This is called informal prayer. It allows us to talk to God sincerely about ourselves, offering to him our particular joys and sorrows and asking him for the special help we need.

Prayers may be said for four reasons. Prayers that primarily acknowledge God's greatness and our dependence on him are prayers of *adoration*. While all of our prayers should begin as prayers of praise, some, such as the *Sanctus* (Holy, Holy, Holy) of the Mass are solely prayers of adoration. The second reason for prayer is to give thanks to God for the blessings he has given us. These are prayers of *thanksgiving*. We are reminded of the importance of giving thanks during each Mass. Before the Eucharistic Prayer the priest proclaims, "Let us give thanks to the Lord our God", to which we reply, "It is right to give him thanks and praise." *Contrition* is the third reason for prayer. In a prayer of contrition we acknowledge our sins and pray to obtain forgiveness from God. When we say the *Confiteor* (I Confess) at the beginning of Mass we are saying a prayer of contrition. The last reason for prayer is *petition*. This is the most common prayer; in fact, many people only remember to pray to God when they need something. Prayers of petition are those in which we ask God for blessings for ourselves and others. It is fitting that we should ask for God's help, since we do need it for our life on earth and in order to reach Heaven. The *Prayers of the Faithful* during Mass are examples of prayers of petition.

Let us now consider some of the formal prayers that are important in the Catholic Church.

First in importance are those prayers that are part of the Church's liturgy—the Mass and the Liturgy of the Hours. The Mass is the perfect prayer, because it is the offering of Christ to his Father in Heaven. The Mass is also the supreme act of worship, by which we thank God. Because the Mass is the same sacrifice as that of Calvary, it is the perfect means of making satisfaction for our sins. Since the Mass is in memory of the Resurrection, it is a prayer of thanksgiving. Finally, since the Mass is the perfect sacrifice, it is the best way of petitioning God.

The Liturgy of the Hours is also an important prayer. It is a prayer of praise, by which we can sanctify our entire day. As we have seen, certain members of the Church—priests and religious—are required to pray the Divine Office each day. But we also are invited by the Church to join in this prayer.

One day the disciples said to Jesus, "Lord, teach us to pray", and he taught them the *Our Father*, or *Lord's Prayer*. This prayer contains an outline of all the qualities that should be present in our prayers and all those things that we should ask of God. Hence, it is not just a wonderful prayer, it is also a model for all of our prayers. It is so rich in meaning that we could meditate on it all our lives. Let us briefly examine the statements found in the Our Father.

Our Father, who art in Heaven,

We begin this prayer by placing ourselves in the presence of God, recognizing him as our *Father*, but also as God.

hallowed be thy name,

Next we adore God, as we ask that his name be made holy and honored on earth.

thy Kingdom come,

We pray that his Kingdom—the Kingdom of Christ, the Church—may grow and be spread throughout the earth.

thy will be done. . . .

We end the first half of this prayer asking that God's will—not ours—be done. To all three of these first petitions we add *"on earth as it is in Heaven"*, for God's name is honored in Heaven; in Heaven his Kingdom has been spread; and finally, in Heaven his will is done.

Give us this day our daily bread,

We pray now for ourselves, asking God to give us the things we need—both physical and spiritual.

*and forgive us our trespasses
as we forgive those who
trespass against us.*

We acknowledge our sins and ask that God in his mercy forgive us in the same measure as we have forgiven those who offend us.

*Lead us not into temptation,
but deliver us from evil.*

We end the prayer asking God to help us in times of temptation and to strengthen us when we face occasions of sin.

Another great prayer that the Church especially recommends is the *Rosary*. This prayer has been part of the spiritual life of many Catholics—mainly in the Latin rite—for almost eight centuries. The Church has encouraged us to say this beautiful prayer by dedicating one month—October—to the Rosary. The Rosary combines both mental and vocal prayer. It is divided into fifteen mysteries, or episodes, from the lives of Jesus and Mary. As we recite the vocal prayers—one Our Father, ten Hail Marys, and one Glory Be for each mystery—we meditate on the various events from the lives of Our Lord and his Mother.

It is important to develop times for prayer in our lives, so that we may fulfill our call to holiness. In the next chapter we will consider the sacraments that further nourish our spiritual life.

Words to Know:

mental prayer   vocal prayer
Rosary   Divine Office

Q. 64   *What is prayer?*
Prayer is a lifting of the soul to God, to know him better, to adore him, to thank him, and to ask him for what we need.

Q. 65   *How many kinds of prayer are there?*
There are two kinds of prayer, mental and vocal.

Q. 66   *What is mental prayer?*
Mental prayer is that which is said interiorly, with mind and heart alone.

Q. 67   *What is vocal prayer?*
Vocal prayer is said by spoken words with the participation of the mind and the heart.

Q. 68 *How should one pray?*

He who prays should do so reflecting that he stands in the presence of the Infinite Majesty of God and has need of his mercy; he should be humble, attentive, and devout in his prayer.

Q. 69 *What things should we ask from God?*

We should ask from God his own glory, and for ourselves we should ask eternal life and graces and also temporal good, as Jesus Christ has taught us in the *Our Father*.

Q. 70 *What is the Our Father?*

The Our Father is the prayer taught and recommended by Jesus Christ, called therefore the Lord's Prayer, the most excellent of all prayers.

Q. 71 *Why is the Our Father the most excellent prayer?*

The Our Father is the most excellent prayer because it came forth from the mind and heart of Jesus, and because it includes in seven brief requests everything we should ask from God as his sons and as brothers to each other.

Q. 72 *What should we ask as good children of God?*

As good children of God we should ask that all men come to know him, that all honor his name, that his kingdom, the Church, be propagated, and that his most Holy Will be fulfilled by all men. This is what we ask in the first three requests of the Our Father.

Q. 73 *As brothers to each other what should we ask?*

As brothers to each other we should ask for bodily and spiritual nourishment, for the pardon of sins, for protection against temptations, and for deliverance from evil. This is what we ask for ourselves and for all men in the last four requests made in the Our Father.

132

CHAPTER 24

The Sacramental Life

". . . Whoever drinks of the water that I shall give him will never thirst; the water that I shall give him will become in him a spring of water welling up to eternal life" (Jn 4:14).

In addition to prayer, Christ has given us a wonderful means to become holy. The *sacraments* were given to the Church by Jesus Christ to sanctify us. They are the means by which we receive the "living water" of which Our Lord spoke. Water in this sense signifies the life of God called *sanctifying grace*.

A sacrament is an outward sign instituted by Christ to give us grace. A *sign* is a thing that stands for, or represents, something else. For example, our national flag represents our country; smoke indicates the presence of fire. We are all familiar with the signs in the sacraments. The water in Baptism, for example, indicates our death to sin, the cleansing of the soul, and the new life which is given by God. But the sacraments are more than ordinary signs. They are *efficacious* signs. This means that they actually bring about what they represent.

To understand this better, think about the ordinary stop sign. This sign indicates to the driver that he should stop at an intersection. But it cannot *make* him stop; he must stop himself. The sacraments are different. In Baptism when the water is poured and the words

"I baptize you . . ." are spoken, the soul is actually cleansed and the new life of grace is actually infused. This is the great power that Our Lord gave to these simple signs.

Christ himself gave us the sacraments so that we could share in his life and have that life nourished in us. He gave us these sacraments so that we would have a certain, or sure, way to receive the grace he won by dying on the Cross for us. But why did he choose to give us this grace through the sacraments?

As human beings we learn through *corporeal*, material, things around us. Thus, to learn we depend on our senses—sight, hearing, touch, taste, and smell. Our Lord gave us the sacraments as *sensible* means—means that can be sensed—for us to know that grace is active in our lives. At Baptism, when we see the water being poured and hear the words, we know that God's life now dwells in the soul of the person baptized. We are certain of this. In the same way, when we hear the priest in Confession say that our sins are forgiven, we *know* that God has forgiven our sins.

All of the sacraments make us holy by giving us grace or by restoring or increasing the life of grace in us. Thus all of the sacraments nourish and strengthen our spiritual life and help us draw closer to God. However, two of the sacraments are our "lifelines" to grace—Penance and the Holy Eucharist.

The Sacrament of Penance

On the evening of the Resurrection, Our Lord appeared to the apostles in the upper room. He said to them, "Receive the Holy Spirit. If you forgive the sins of any, they are forgiven; if you retain the sins of any, they are retained" (Jn 20:22–23). Christ gave the apostles and their successors the power to forgive sins, thus instituting the sacrament of Penance, or Confession.

Although original sin is removed through the sacrament of Baptism, we know that we are still in a weakened state. We have a strong inclination to sin, and we do, in fact, easily fall into sin. Our Lord knew that even after Baptism Christians could still sin. He gave us the sacrament of Penance or Reconciliation so that we could receive God's forgiveness frequently.

The sacrament of Penance, then, is a great gift by which the sins we commit after Baptism are forgiven. If we have committed a mortal sin, God restores to our soul his life which had been lost. God increases his life within us and strengthens our friendship with him when we confess our venial sins. In addition, through the actual or sacramental graces which we receive, God helps us to avoid sin in the future. For example, if you confess that you have lied, God will give you strength and help you be truthful in the future.

The sacrament of Penance can help us draw closer to God and make us better and stronger Christians. For this reason, it is good to receive this sacrament often—even when we have not committed any mortal sins.

To make a good Confession and worthily receive the sacrament we must do five things:

1. Before receiving the sacrament you must examine your conscience. You should ask God to help you recognize your sins since your last confession.

2. You must have true sorrow, *contrition*, for your sins. This contrition is based on our love of God, sorrow for having offended him, and hatred of our sins.

3. You must have a firm commitment not to sin again. This means that you must resolve to do all you can to avoid sin and the occasions of sin in the future. If you do not intend to give up your sinful ways, God cannot forgive you. You would not be truly sorry.

4. You must confess your sins honestly to the priest. This means that you should not conceal any mortal sins. Neither should you try to hide anything out of shame or embarrassment. The priest, taking the place of Christ, is there to give you forgiveness and not to rebuke you unnecessarily. He may, however, give you some advice or guidance to help you overcome your sins.

5. You must be willing to perform the penance which the priest gives you and then to do it.

"I am the Bread of Life. He who comes to me will never be hungry; he who believes in me will never thirst."

(John 6:35)

"... this is the Bread that comes down from Heaven so that a man may eat it and not die." *(John 6:50)*

The Holy Eucharist

"Truly, truly, I say to you . . . he who eats my flesh and drinks my blood, has eternal life. . ." (Jn 6:54).

The Eucharist is the sacrament in which Our Lord is present—Body and Blood, soul and divinity—under the appearances of bread and wine. Just as our bodies need physical nourishment in order to live, our souls also must be nourished. The Eucharist is this spiritual food.

The Eucharist is a means of receiving grace and, at the same time, is the source of grace—Jesus, himself. The Eucharist is thus the most important sacrament and the fountain from which all grace flows.

In receiving the Eucharist—called Holy Communion—we become united to Christ. This union nourishes us by helping us to become more like Christ. Through reception of Communion the life of God is increased in our souls, bringing us closer to him. Just as food strengthens our bodies for difficult physical tasks, this great Sacrament helps us to become spiritually stronger.

To benefit from the graces of the Eucharist we must prepare ourselves to receive it worthily. First we must be in the state of grace when we receive Holy Communion. This means that if we have committed a mortal sin we must first go to Confession before receiving Our Lord. St. Paul told the Christians at Corinth: "Whoever . . . eats the Bread or drinks the Cup of the Lord in an unworthy manner will be guilty of profaning the Body and Blood of the Lord" (1 Cor 11:27). To receive Our Lord in the state of serious sin is a sin of sacrilege.

Secondly, to receive the Eucharist worthily we must believe that Jesus Christ is truly present in the sacrament. Again St. Paul reminds us: ". . . anyone who eats and drinks without discerning the Body eats and drinks judgment upon himself" (1 Cor 11:29). We must, then, prepare ourselves to receive Communion by remembering that we are about to receive the Body and Blood of Our Lord.

Finally, we must observe the Eucharistic fast. The Church gives us this law—no food or drink (except water or medicine) for one hour before receiving Communion—out of reverence so that we may prepare ourselves to receive our great Lord and King. This small sacrifice reminds us of what we are about to do. (The sick and those who care for them are exempt from this fast.)

After we receive Our Lord, we should spend time in *thanksgiving*—thanking him for coming to us and asking Jesus to help us. The following prayer, called the *Anima Christi*, might help us meditate on the great gift we receive. Many people recite this prayer after Communion.

Soul of Christ, sanctify me.
Body of Christ, save me.
Blood of Christ, inebriate me.
Water from the side of Christ, wash me.
Passion of Christ, strengthen me.
O Good Jesus, hear me.
Within thy wounds, hide me.
Suffer me not to be separated from thee.
From the malicious enemy, defend me.
In the hour of death, call me.
And bid me come to thee, that with thy
saints I may praise thee for ever and
ever. *Amen.*

> "According to his riches may he grant you to be strengthened with might through his Spirit in the inner man, and may Christ dwell in your hearts through faith; that you, being rooted and grounded in love, may have power to comprehend with all the saints what is the breadth and length and height and depth, and to know the love of Christ which surpasses knowledge, that you may be filled with all the fulness of God."
>
> (Ephesians 3:16–19)

Because the Eucharist is our source of spiritual nourishment, it is good to receive this sacrament frequently. By attending Mass each Sunday we are able to receive Holy Communion at least once a week. However, realizing the greatness of this sacrament, we should try to receive Our Lord even more often—even daily —by attending Mass during the week. St. Francis de Sales, in his *Introduction to the Devout Life*, reminds us of this.

> Two classes of people should communicate often, the perfect because, being well prepared, they would be very wrong not to approach the fountainhead of perfection; and the imperfect, that they might preserve their strength; the weak that they might become strong; the sick that they might find a cure; the healthy, that they might be preserved from sickness.

Even when we are unable to attend Mass we can make a *spiritual communion* in which we ask Our Lord to come to us and dwell in us in a special way.

When we pray, "Give us this day our daily bread", we include asking to receive the Eucharist. When we realize the extreme love for us which Jesus showed in establishing a way to stay with us on earth, we will long to receive him as often as possible. He was the delight of the saints. St. Teresa of Avila prayed that "though our bodily eyes cannot feast themselves on the sight of him since he is hidden from us, he may reveal himself to the eyes of the soul and may make himself known to us as another kind of food, full of delight and joy, which sustains our life."

St. Bonaventure prays: "Grant that my soul may hunger after you . . . upon whom the angels desire to look, and may my inmost soul be filled with the sweetness of your savor; may it ever thirst for you, the fountain of life, the foundation of wisdom and knowledge, the fountain of eternal light, the torrent of pleasure, the richness of the house of God."

In addition to the reception of Our Lord in the Eucharist, we can adore him and draw closer to him through adoration of the Blessed Sacrament. The *Real Presence* of Christ in the Eucharist remains after Mass. Therefore consecrated Hosts are reserved in the tabernacle in the church. Because Christ is truly present in our churches and chapels, we should try to spend time adoring him, thanking him, and talking to him about our needs. If we cannot get to daily Mass, perhaps we can make a daily visit to Our Lord in the Blessed Sacrament.

Besides such visits, there are sometimes special devotions to the Blessed Sacrament in which we can participate. We may go to church for *Benediction*. The Eucharist is placed in a special container called a *monstrance*, so that we may see and adore the Body of Christ. The priest holds up the monstrance and blesses us with Christ himself. Sometimes the Host in the monstrance will be exposed on our altars throughout the day so that we may pray to Our Lord in a special way.

These devotions remind us of Christ's presence in the Eucharist and help us draw closer to him. We can deepen our union with Christ by receiving Communion often and visiting him in the Blessed Sacrament.

Words to Know:

sacrament   Eucharist   grace
Benediction   monstrance

Q. 74 *What are the sacraments?*
The sacraments are efficacious signs of grace instituted by Jesus Christ to make us holy.

Q. 75 *How do the sacraments make us holy?*
The sacraments make us holy either by giving us the first sanctifying grace which takes away sin or by increasing that grace which we already possess.

Q. 76 *What should we do to preserve the grace of the sacraments?*
To preserve the grace of the sacraments we must cooperate by our way of living, doing good, and avoiding evil.

Q. 77 *What is Confession?*
Confession (Penance or Reconciliation) is the sacrament instituted by Jesus Christ to forgive the sins committed after Baptism.

Q. 78 *How many things are required to make a good Confession?*
To make a good Confession five things are required: (1) examination of conscience; (2) sorrow for sins; (3) the intention of not committing sin again; (4) the accusation of our sin; (5) satisfaction or penance.

Q. 79 *How is the examination of conscience done?*

The examination of conscience is done by recalling to mind the sins we have committed in thoughts, words, and omissions against the Commandments of God, against the precepts of the Church, and against the obligations of our own state in life, beginning from the last good Confession.

Q. 80 *What is the Eucharist?*

The Eucharist is the sacrament which contains really present the Body, Blood, soul, and divinity of Our Lord Jesus Christ, under the appearances of bread and wine, for the nourishment of souls.

Q. 81 *Is the same Jesus Christ present in the Eucharist who was born on earth of the Virgin Mary?*

Yes, the same Jesus Christ is present in the Eucharist who is in Heaven, and who was born on earth of the Virgin Mary.

Q. 82 *What things are necessary for the worthy reception of Holy Communion?*

For a worthy reception of Holy Communion three things are necessary: first, to be in the grace of God; second, to realize and to consider whom we are about to receive; third, to observe the Eucharistic fast.

Q. 83 *Is it a good and useful thing to receive Holy Communion frequently?*

It is a very good thing and most useful to receive Holy Communion frequently, even every day, provided it is done always with the right dispositions.

Prayer After Communion

''My Lord Jesus Christ, I believe that you are truly within me with your Body, Blood, soul and divinity; humbled in my nothingness, I adore you profoundly as my God and my Lord.''

PART FOUR

The End of Christian Life

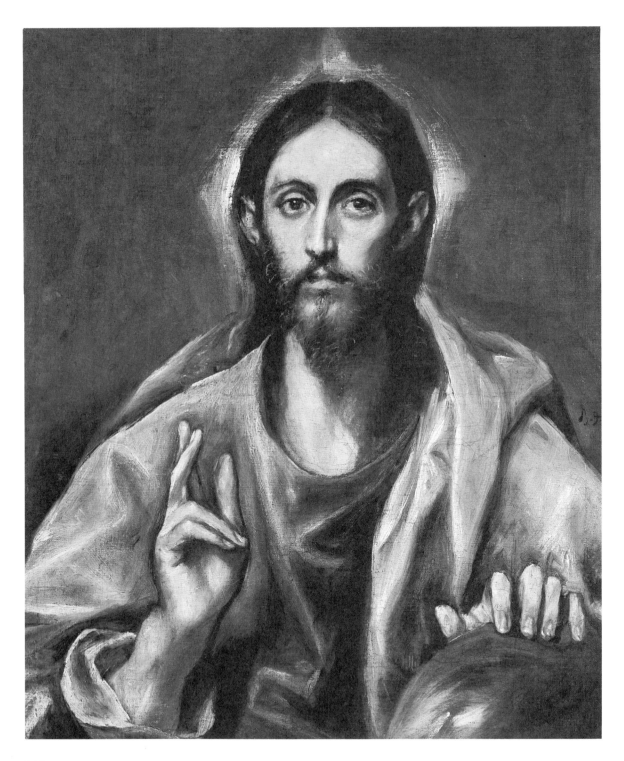

140

CHAPTER 25

Death and the Particular Judgment

"Remember, man, that you are dust and to dust you will return."

These words are said each year on Ash Wednesday to remind us of our mortality. Each of us will eventually die. This is one of the consequences for all living, material creatures. Plants and animals eventually die; even inanimate, non-living, objects do not last forever. Human beings, since we are mortal, must eventually die, a result of original sin.

Although the separation of body and soul—death—is inevitable, we know that there is life beyond the grave. Human beings have a mortal body but an *immortal* soul. Because of this we see that death is not really the end of life but only the end of this life. In the Preface used at Masses for the dead we are reminded that for the Christian "life is not ended but merely changed".

Our faith tells us that death is the gateway to life with God. In the Gospel, Martha, the sister of Lazarus, showed us how Christians ought to understand death. When Our Lord came to Bethany after Lazarus' death, Martha said to Him: "I know that [my brother] will rise again in the resurrection on the last day" (Jn 11:24).

Since death will come for each of us, what should be our attitude toward it? Our Lord tells us that we should prepare ourselves for death. We should remember the parable about the servants who are awaiting their master's return. Since they do not know exactly when he will come, they must prepare themselves. We must also be prepared:

> Watch therefore—for [we] do not know when the master of the house will come, in the evening, or at midnight, or at cockcrow, or in the morning. . . (Mk 13:35).

How can we prepare ourselves for death? We prepare throughout our lives by growing in faith and love. The best preparation for death is to live according to God's will, developing our spiritual lives through prayer and the sacraments. Whenever we pray the Hail Mary we ask our Mother in Heaven to pray for us "now and at the hour of our death". Following our vocation and generously serving God will prepare us for death and our meeting with Christ. We should pray that we may receive the sacraments before our death. By the sacrament of Anointing, dangerously ill persons are commended to the Lord, that he may support and save them.

"Whoever sees the Son and believes in him shall have eternal life and I shall raise him up on the last day" *(John 6:40)*.

Hopefully, we will also be able to receive the sacrament of Penance and the Eucharist as Viaticum.

When we die we will meet Our Lord and be judged by him. The *particular judgment* occurs at the moment of our death and will be based on those things which we did or neglected to do in this life. At this judgment we will see ourselves as we are—our sins and failings, as well as our virtues. We will also see the perfect justice of God's judgment. For this reason it is extremely important to develop the habit of appealing to God's mercy for us sinners. This appeal, made habitually, will bring down his mercy on us and others for that moment when we so critically need it. By remembering what St. Paul said we will prepare for this great moment:

> He will render to every man according to his works: to those who by patience in well-doing seek for glory and honor and immortality, he will give eternal life; but for those who are factious and do not obey the truth, but obey wickedness, there will be wrath and fury (Rom 2:6—8).

At the particular judgment those who have died in the state of mortal sin—without repenting —will be separated from God for ever. They will suffer eternal punishment because of their own actions and choice. In the parable of the rich man (Dives) and Lazarus Our Lord reminded us of the permanence of this state (Lk 16:19—31). Once one is in Hell, there is no chance for repentance. While the souls of the damned suffer sensible pain, the greatest suffering in Hell is the loss of God. They will be without hope, knowing that their own rejection of God is the cause of their damnation.

It is good to remember that God does not want anyone to suffer in Hell. In fact, he did not create Hell for man. The angels who rebelled were banished from God's sight and this is Hell. God created man, like the angels, with a free will. Thus, if we should turn away from him, we will join the fallen angels in suffering this eternal punishment.

Some who die are not in the state of mortal sin, but still have venial sins which they have not fully repented of or done adequate penance for. Because these people have not completely separated themselves from God, they will not go to Hell. They will go first to *Purgatory*. Here they will be prepared for Heaven. The doctrine of Purgatory is very consoling since, because of God's mercy, we can be saved even though we are not perfect. We can go through a time of purification. Even though it is a painful suffering, we are full of hope.

Other people whose love for God is perfect will go straight to Heaven. The reward for the just is *eternal life* in which they will enjoy the vision of God. This is called the *Beatific Vision*. In Heaven "we shall see [God] as he is" (1 Jn 3:2). It is this which gives us true happiness. In Heaven, we will know God as completely as we can:

> Now we see in a mirror dimly, but then face to face. Now I know in part; then I shall understand fully. . . (1 Cor 13:12).

Here we will be able perfectly to love God and others.

We know that Heaven will bring us great joy, and yet it is difficult for us to grasp what it is really like. St. Paul tells us:

No eye has seen, nor ear heard, nor the heart of man conceived, what God has prepared for those who love him (1 Cor 2:9).

Heaven will be far greater than anything we can imagine. It will encompass all those things which are truly good.

Besides the great joy of the Beatific Vision, there will be other joys in Heaven. In Heaven there will be no sorrow or pain as St. John tells us in the book of Revelation:

He will wipe away every tear from their eyes . . . neither shall there be mourning nor crying nor pain any more. . . (Rev 21:4).

There will also be no more sin or temptation in Heaven. The struggle will be over and peace will remain. We will be united with the angels, the saints, and those we have known and loved on earth.

Since we cannot really understand much of what Heaven is like, we may sometimes be tempted to think that it will be boring. Yet boredom is an imperfection of life on earth and cannot be part of life in Heaven. If boredom is a part of life after death, it is part of life in Hell, not Heaven. Although the many particulars of life in Heaven are unknown, we should remember the words of St. Paul—Heaven is beyond our wildest dreams!

We should begin now by preparing ourselves for the day when Christ will call us to come home and be with him. We want to be able to say the words which St. Paul wrote near the end of his life, in a letter to Timothy:

As for me, my life is already being poured away as a libation, and the time has come for me to be gone. I have fought the good fight to the end; I have run the race to the finish; I have kept the faith; all there is to come now is the crown of righteousness reserved for me, which the Lord, the righteous Judge, will give to me on that Day; and not only to me but all those who have longed for his appearing (2 Tim 4:6−8).

Words to Know:

Particular Judgment   Beatific Vision
immortal

CHAPTER 26

The Trumpet Shall Sound—
The End of the World

At the Ascension of Our Lord into Heaven, two angels spoke to the apostles saying:

> *"Why do you stand looking into Heaven? This Jesus, who was taken up from you into Heaven, will come in the same way as you saw him go into Heaven" (Acts 1:11).*

In the Nicene Creed we say that Jesus "will come again in glory to judge the living and the dead". When Christ first came among us, he came in poverty, humility, and weakness. He was born in a stable fit for animals, not a King. He was God, but he took on human nature and began his life in the most humble state—as a baby. He was God, but he took on the weaknesses of human nature—except sin—in order to teach us. When Christ comes again—the *Second Coming*—at the end of the world, he will come in triumph, as the King and Judge of the world. He will come in glory and be recognized by all men as Christ the King.

The time when this will occur is unknown. When the apostles asked Our Lord about the end of the world (Mt 24), he spoke of various signs and warnings which would precede the event. He said that there would be wars and rumors of wars, famines, false prophets, and persecutions. All of these, however, have occurred at various times in history. And many individuals in the past (as well as the present) have mistaken the troubles of their own times as signs of the end of the world. But they neglected Our Lord's final words about the end, which are the most important:

> But of that day and hour no one knows, not even the angels of Heaven . . . only the Father. . . (Mt 24:36).

Just as we do not know when the world will end, we do not know exactly how it will end either. It is possible that the end of the world will be caused by humans, for example through war or the misuse of natural resources. But it is also possible that God will directly bring about the end of the world. However, it will not take place until God wills it.

At the end of the world Our Lord will judge the entire human race. This is known as the General Judgment and is described by Our Lord in the Gospel of Matthew (Mt 25). At that time Christ will judge both those who are alive at the end and those who have already died. All of our deeds—even secret ones—will be made known. Everyone will recognize the holiness of the just and understand why they have been rewarded. We will also see God's justice in the condemnation of unrepentant sinners who will be banished for eternity to Hell. There will be no changes in the judgment for those who have already died. But now, however, their judgment will be made known to all.

The *Dies Irae* (which means "day of wrath") is a Latin poem which was written many centuries ago and sung on All Souls' Day and at Masses for the dead. It reminds us of this day of final judgment. Below are two verses which illustrate what will occur at the last judgment:

> Then the volume shall be spread
> And the writing shall be read
> Which shall judge the quick and dead.

> When the Judge his place has ta'en
> All things shall be made plain
> Nothing unavenged remain.

Those who have loved God and served him on this earth will stand on his right. They will be rewarded with Heaven. Those who have turned away from God will stand on the left and will be banished for ever to Hell. There will no longer be any need for Purgatory at the end of the world. Those souls who are in Purgatory at the end will go to Heaven. All the wisdom, justice, mercy and loving kindness of God in his dealings with men will be made known. Our Lord Jesus Christ will be fully glorified. He will appear in splendor and triumph. Evil will be completely overcome. The reign of God will be complete.

> We shall not all sleep, but we shall all be changed, in a moment, in the twinkling of an eye, at the last trumpet. For the trumpet will sound, and the dead will be raised imperishably and we shall be changed. For this perishable nature must put on the imperishable, and this mortal nature must put on immortality (1 Cor 15:51−53).

At the end of the world, also, our human natures will once again be complete. Our bodies will be reunited with our souls, because man is both body and soul. This is called the *resurrection of the body*. We will enjoy the glories of Heaven or suffer the pains of Hell as a complete human being—body and soul.

The bodies of the just will be glorified in Heaven. This means that our bodies will be perfected as was Our Lord's body after the Resurrection. Theologians have distinguished four properties or gifts which will belong to the glorified body. The glorified body will be incapable of physical suffering and will be free from death. This is known as *impassibility*, which comes from the Latin word "to suffer". Our bodies will have the property of *subtlety*, which means that our spiritual nature will shine through the body instead of being hidden by it. Thirdly, the glorified body will possess *agility*, which means that the body will be able to obey the soul with great ease and speed. This was manifested by the risen Christ, who quickly disappeared from the midst of the apostles (Jn 20:19, 26). Finally our resurrected bodies will have *clarity*. They will be free from all deformities—even minor ones—and will be filled with beauty.

Even the earth will be transformed in some way. St. John had a vision of the transformation of all things which he tells us in the book of Revelation:

> Then I saw a new Heaven and new earth; for the first Heaven and the first earth had passed away, and the sea was no more. And I saw the holy city, new Jerusalem, coming down out of Heaven from God . . . and I heard a great voice from the throne saying, "Behold, the dwelling of God is with men. He will dwell with them, and they shall be his people. . ." (Rev 21:1−3).

All of this is the perfect happiness which awaits us. God has prepared this for us. We must spend our lives preparing for this so that we may enjoy the blessings of Heaven for eternity.

Words to Know:

second coming   General Judgment

"When the Son of Man comes in his glory, and all the angels with him, then he will sit on his glorious throne. Before him will be gathered all the nations. . . . Then the King will say to those on his right hand, 'Come, O blessed of my Father, inherit the Kingdom prepared for you from the foundation of the world; for I was hungry and you gave me food, I was thirsty and you gave me drink, I was a stranger and you welcomed me, I was naked and you clothed me, I was sick and you visited me, I was in prison and you came to me.'. . . Then he will say to those on his left hand, 'Depart from me you cursed, into eternal fire prepared for the devil and his angels, for I was hungry and you gave me no food, thirsty and you gave me no drink. . . .'"

(Matthew 25:31−42)

Appendix

PRAYERS

THE SIGN OF THE CROSS

In the name of the Father, and of the Son, and of the Holy Spirit. *Amen.*

OUR FATHER

Our Father who art in Heaven, hallowed be thy Name. Thy Kingdom come, thy will be done on earth as it is in Heaven. Give us this day our daily bread, and forgive us our trespasses, as we forgive those who trespass against us, and lead us not into temptation, but deliver us from evil. *Amen.*

HAIL MARY

Hail Mary, full of grace, the Lord is with thee. Blessed art thou among women, and blessed is the fruit of thy womb, Jesus.

Holy Mary, Mother of God, pray for us sinners now and at the hour of our death. *Amen.*

GLORY BE

Glory be to the Father, and to the Son, and to the Holy Spirit. As it was in the beginning, is now, and ever shall be, world without end. *Amen.*

MORNING OFFERING

O Jesus, through the Immaculate Heart of Mary I offer thee my prayers, works, joys, and sufferings of this day in union with the Holy Sacrifice of the Mass throughout the world. I offer them for all the intentions of thy Sacred Heart: the salvation of souls, reparation for sin, the reunion of all Christians. I offer them for the intentions of our Bishops and of all Apostles of Prayer, and in particular for those recommended by our Holy Father this month.

THE APOSTLES' CREED

I believe in God, the Father Almighty, Creator of Heaven and earth; and in Jesus Christ, his only Son, Our Lord, who was conceived by the Holy Spirit, born of the Virgin Mary, suffered under Pontius Pilate, was crucified, died, and was buried. He descended into Hell; the third day he rose again from the dead. He ascended into Heaven, and is seated at the right hand of God, the Father almighty. From thence he shall come to judge the living and the dead.

I believe in the Holy Spirit, the Holy Catholic Church, the Communion of Saints, the forgiveness of sins, the resurrection of the body, and life everlasting. *Amen.*

ACT OF CONTRITION

O my God, I am heartily sorry for having offended thee. I detest all my sins because of thy just punishments, but most of all because they offend thee, my God, who art all good and deserving of all my love. I firmly resolve, with the help of thy grace, to confess my sins, to do penance, and to amend my life. *Amen.*

ACT OF FAITH

O my God, I firmly believe that thou art one God in three Divine Persons, Father, Son, and Holy Spirit; I believe that thy Divine Son became man and died for our sins, and that he will come to judge the living and the dead. I believe these and all the truths that the Holy Catholic Church teaches, because thou hast revealed them, who can neither deceive nor be deceived.

ACT OF HOPE

O my God, relying on thy infinite goodness and promises, I hope to obtain pardon of my sins, the help of thy grace, and life everlasting, through the merits of Jesus Christ, my Lord and Redeemer.

ACT OF LOVE

O my God, I love thee above all things, with my whole heart and soul, because thou art all good and worthy of all love. I love my neighbor as myself for the love of thee. I forgive all who have injured me and ask pardon of all whom I have injured.

MYSTERIES OF THE ROSARY

The Joyful Mysteries

1. The Annunciation.
2. The Visitation.
3. The Nativity.
4. The Presentation.
5. The Finding in the Temple.

The Sorrowful Mysteries

1. The Agony in the Garden.
2. The Scourging at the Pillar.
3. The Crowning with Thorns.
4. The Carrying of the Cross.
5. The Crucifixion.

The Glorious Mysteries

1. The Resurrection.
2. The Ascension.
3. The Descent of the Holy Spirit.
4. The Assumption.
5. The Coronation.

THE STATIONS OF THE CROSS

1. Jesus is condemned to death.
2. Jesus carries his Cross.
3. Jesus falls the first time.
4. Jesus meets his Mother.
5. Jesus is helped by Simon of Cyrene.
6. Veronica wipes the face of Jesus.
7. Jesus falls a second time.
8. Jesus speaks to the women.
9. Jesus falls a third time.
10. Jesus is stripped of his clothes.
11. Jesus is nailed to the Cross.
12. Jesus dies on the Cross.
13. Jesus is taken down from the Cross.
14. Jesus is placed in the tomb.

THE ANGELUS

V. *The angel of the Lord declared unto Mary.*
R. And she conceived of the Holy Spirit.
   Hail Mary. . . .

V. *Behold the handmaid of the Lord.*
R. Be it done to me according to thy word.
   Hail Mary. . . .

V. *And the Word was made flesh.*
R. And dwelt among us.
   Hail Mary. . . .

V. *Pray for us, O holy Mother of God.*
R. That we may be made worthy of the promises of Christ.

Let us pray. Pour forth, we beseech thee, O Lord, thy grace into our hearts, that we, to whom the Incarnation of Christ thy Son was made known by the message of an angel, may by his Passion and Cross be brought to the glory of his Resurrection. Through the same Christ Our Lord. *Amen.*

LITANY OF THE BLESSED VIRGIN MARY

Lord, have mercy.
Christ, have mercy.
Lord, have mercy.
Christ, hear us.
Christ, graciously hear us.
God, the Father of Heaven,
   have mercy on us.
God the Son, Redeemer of
the world,
   have mercy on us.
God the Holy Spirit,
   have mercy on us.
Holy Trinity, One God,
   have mercy on us.
Holy Mary, *pray for us* [*]
Holy Mother of God,
Holy Virgin of virgins,
Mother of Christ,
Mother of divine grace,
Mother most pure,
Mother most chaste,
Mother inviolate,
Mother undefiled,
Mother most amiable,
Mother most admirable,
Mother of good counsel,
Mother of our Creator,
Mother of our Savior,
Virgin most prudent,
Virgin most venerable,
Virgin most renowned,
Virgin most powerful,
Virgin most merciful,
Virgin most faithful,
Mirror of justice,
Seat of wisdom,
Cause of our joy,

Spiritual vessel,
Vessel of honor,
Singular Vessel of devotion,
Mystical rose,
Tower of David,
Tower of ivory,
House of gold,
Ark of the Covenant,
Gate of heaven,
Morning star,
Health of the sick,
Refuge of sinners,
Comforter of the afflicted,
Help of Christians,
Queen of Angels,
Queen of Patriarchs,
Queen of Prophets,
Queen of Apostles,
Queen of Martyrs,
Queen of Confessors,
Queen of Virgins,
Queen of all Saints,
Queen conceived without original sin,
Queen assumed into Heaven,
Queen of the most holy Rosary,
Queen of Peace,

Lamb of God, who take away the sins of the
   world, *spare us, O Lord!*
Lamb of God, who take away the sins of the
   world, *graciously hear us, O Lord!*
Lamb of God, who take away the sins of the
   world, *have mercy on us.*

Pray for us, O holy Mother of God.
That we may be made worthy of the promises
   of Christ.

[*]*Pray for us* is repeated after each invocation.

PRAYER FOR THE POPE

Father of Providence, look with love on N. our Pope, your appointed successor to St. Peter on whom you built your Church. May he be the visible center and foundation of our unity in faith and love. Grant this through Our Lord Jesus Christ, your Son, who lives and reigns with you and the Holy Spirit, one God, for ever and ever. *Amen.*

PRAYER FOR A BISHOP

Lord our God, you have chosen your servant N. to be a shepherd of your flock in the tradition of the apostles. Give him a spirit of courage and right judgment, a spirit of knowledge and love. By governing with fidelity those entrusted to his care may he build your Church as a sign of salvation for the world. We ask this through Our Lord Jesus Christ, your Son, who lives and reigns with you and the Holy Spirit, one God, for ever and ever. *Amen.*

PRAYER FOR VOCATIONS
by POPE JOHN PAUL II

O Jesus, our Good Shepherd, bless all our parishes with numerous priests, deacons, men and women in religious life, consecrated laity and missionaries, according to the needs of the entire world, which you love and wish to save.

We especially entrust our community to you; grant us the spirit of the first Christians, so that we may be a cenacle of prayer, in loving acceptance of the Holy Spirit and his gifts.

Assist our pastors and all who live a consecrated life. Guide the steps of those who have responded generously to your call and are preparing to receive holy orders or to profess the evangelical counsels.

Look with love on so many well-disposed young people and call them to follow you. Help them to understand that in you alone can they attain to complete fulfillment.

To this end we call on the powerful intercession of Mary, Mother and Model of all vocations. We beseech you to sustain our faith with the certainty that the Father will grant what you have commanded us to ask. *Amen.*

PRAYER FOR UNITY OF THE CHURCH

Almighty and merciful God, you willed that the different nations should become one people through your Son. Grant in your kindness that those who glory in being known as Christians may put aside their differences and become one in truth and charity, and that all men, enlightened by the true faith, may be united in fraternal communion in the one Church. Through Christ Our Lord. *Amen.*

MEMORARE

Remember, O most gracious Virgin Mary, that never was it known that anyone who fled to thy protection, implored thy help, or sought thy intercession, was left unaided. Inspired with this confidence, I fly unto thee, O Virgin of Virgins, my Mother: to thee do I come, before thee I stand, sinful and sorrowful. O Mother of the Word Incarnate, despise not my petitions, but in thy mercy hear and answer me. *Amen*.

PRAYER TO ST. MICHAEL

St. Michael, the Archangel, defend us in battle. Be our protection against the wickedness and snares of the devil. May God rebuke him, we humbly pray, and do thou, O prince of the Heavenly hosts, by the power of God, thrust into Hell Satan and the other evil spirits who prowl about the world seeking the ruin of souls. *Amen*.

ABBREVIATIONS

AA   *Apostolicam actuositatem* (Decree on the Apostolate of the Laity), November 18, 1965.

DH   *Dignitatis humanae* (Declaration on Religious Liberty), December 7, 1965.

DV   *Dei verbum* (Dogmatic Constitution on Divine Revelation), November 18, 1965.

FC   *Familiaris consortio* (The Role of the Christian Family in the Modern World), November 22, 1981.

GS   *Gaudium et Spes* (Pastoral Constitution on the Church in the Modern World), December 7, 1965.

LG   *Lumen Gentium* (Dogmatic Constitution on the Church), November 21, 1964.

MD   *Mediator Dei*, November 20, 1947 (Encyclical of Pius XII).

OE   *Orientalium Ecclesiarum* (Decree on the Catholic Eastern Churches), November 21, 1964.

PC   *Perfectae caritatis* (Decree on the Up-to-date Renewal of Religious Life), October 28, 1965.

SC   *Sacrosanctum concilium* (Constitution on the Sacred Liturgy), December 4, 1963.

UR   *Unitatis redintegratio* (Decree on Ecumenism), November 21, 1964.

ART CREDITS

page ART RESOURCE, NEW YORK

cover *Chair of St. Peter*, photograph by Toni Nicolini (Milan)

10 *Ascension of Christ with the Four Evangelists*, della Porta (Scala)
17 *Conversion of St. Paul*, Caravaggio (Scala)
19 *Apostles*, Chartres, South Portal (Giraudon)
22 *Dispute over the Blessed Sacrament*, Raphael (Scala)
37 *St. Augustine in his Cell*, Botticelli (Scala)
49 *Coronation of the Virgin* (detail), Fra Angelico
54 *Trinity in Glory*, Chantilly (Giraudon)
66 *The Vision of St. Thomas Aquinas* (detail), Sasetta (Scala)
67 *St. Catherine*, Martini (Scala)
68 *St. Ignatius of Loyola*, woodcut (Giraudon)
81 *Cain and Abel*, Titan (Scala)

METROPOLITAN MUSEUM OF ART, NEW YORK

11 *The Dove of the Holy Spirit* (detail from *The Annunciation*, Joos van Cleve); The Friedsam Collection
12 *Pentecost*, Mosan, 12th century; The Cloisters Collection, 1965
78 *Christ Carrying the Cross*, El Greco; the Robert Lehman Collection
107 *Holy Family*, from the church of Gutenzell; gift of Alastair B. Martin, 1948
145 *The Last Judgment*, Jan van Eyck; Fletcher Fund, 1933

NATIONAL GALLERY OF ART, WASHINGTON, D.C.

43 *Enthroned Madonna and Child*, Byzantine; gift of Mrs. Otto H. Kahn
94 *St. Anthony Distributing His Wealth to the Poor*, Sassetta and assistant; Samuel H. Kress Collection
118 *Christ between St. Peter and St. James Major* (detail), follower of Cimabue; Andrew W. Mellon Collection
126 *The Madonna of Humility*, Fra Angelico; Andrew W. Mellon Collection

HISPANIC SOCIETY OF AMERICA, NEW YORK

30 *The Immaculate Conception*, School of Madrid (Jose Antolinez?)
60 *St. Paul*, Jusepe de Ribera

NATIONAL GALLERY OF SCOTLAND, EDINBURGH

140   *Christ, the Savior of the World*, El Greco

PHOTOGRAPHS

Oblates of the Blessed Virgin Mary, Boston: 35, 101
Victor Puccetti: 29, 74, 120
Gary Fuchs: 38,132
Sisters of the Immaculate Heart, Wichita: 99
Spiering: 87
Martha Brown: 108
Fr. Salvatore Fink: 124 (Titus Brandsma)
Stock, Boston:
Herb Snitzer: 72
Bill Gallery: 84
Owen Franken: 103
Milton Feinberg: 104
J. Howard: 110